"A great book on more legends than losers. Thanks to Andy Jones for helping us better understand who we are and where we come from."

Joseph E. Kernan, *Lieutenant Governor, State of Indiana*

"...Even though I feel familiar with our community, I am often asked questions to which I don't know the answer. It sounds like this book will tell us everything we always wanted to know and we will have all the answers."

Ernestine M. Raclin, *Chairman Emeritus, 1st Source Bank*

"Q: Where can you find unique, interesting, fun, and informative factoids about South Bend and its environs?
A: Andy Jones' LEGENDS AND LOSERS."

Stephen J. Luecke, *Mayor, City of South Bend*

"...Packed with challenging and intriguing facts about the people and places of the South Bend - Mishawaka - Notre Dame community."

Robert C. Beutter, *Mayor, City of Mishawaka*

"It is a combination of good fun and a good educational technique, and full of very interesting and surprising information."

Rev. E. William Beauchamp, *C.S.C., Executive Vice President, University of Notre Dame*

"This is a fun book-- entertaining reading for anyone who lives in Michiana or has an interest in it."

Tim Harmon, *Managing Editor, South Bend Tribune*

"The statistics and facts of South Bend and northern Indiana would be difficult to find in other volumes. Your book shows a depth of long hours of study and research.

Violet Schmidt Weitzman, *All-American Girls Baseball League*
(See question number 180)

LEGENDS AND LOSERS

Trivia From the South Bend and Notre Dame Region

Front Cover

In counter-clockwise order beginning with Top Center:

Golden Dome, University of Notre Dame

Hon. William G. George
See question number 13

Violet Schmidt Weitzman
See question number 180

Hilda Koch, Miss Indiana
See question number 61

Council Oak
See question number 121

Vincent Bendix
See question numbers 6, 12, 44, 85, 100, 109, 152

Leopold Pokagon
See question numbers 31, 83

Phyllis Kugler McCormick
See question number 192

Robert Cavelier Sieur de LaSalle
See question numbers 90, 121, 136

Back Cover

Studebaker Proving Grounds, 1932 -- Studebaker Tree Sign
See question number 116

Cover Design: Patty Walsh

LEGENDS AND LOSERS

Trivia From the South Bend and Notre Dame Region

Andy Jones

and books
South Bend, Indiana

LEGENDS AND LOSERS

and books
702 South Michigan, South Bend, Indiana 46601

Library of Congress Catalog Number: 99-62095

International Standard Book Number: 0-89708-221-4

2 3 4 5 6 7 8 9

Printed in the United States of America

Additional copies:

      the distributors
      702 S. Michigan
      South Bend, IN 46601

With much gratitude to my family --
my husband, Duke, and children, Duke, Heather and Lindsey
for their support and patience
while I researched and wrote this book.

And many thanks to my mother-in-law, Nancy Jones, and good friend, Sandra Chrystal Hayes, for their scholarly advice.

Thanks also to the staff of the South Bend and Mishawaka Libraries, Jeanne Denham from the Studebaker National Museum archives, Mary Renshaw from the Northern Indiana Center for History archives, and Tom Cashore from the South Bend Tribune archives.

Map of Region

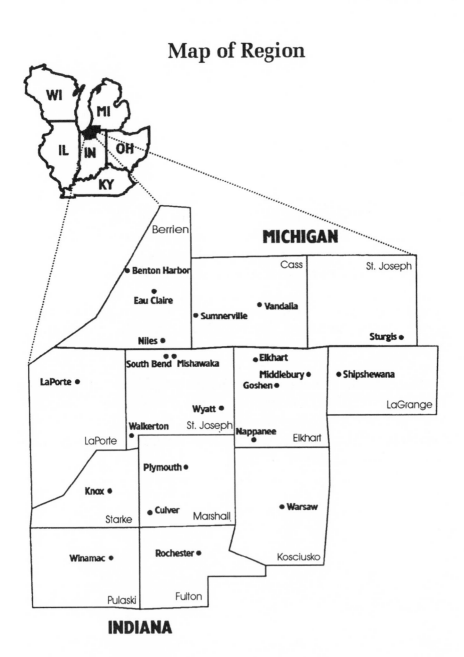

Courtesy of 1ST SOURCE BANK

Behold the work of the old
Let your heritage not be lost
But bequeath it as a memory, treasure and blessing
Gather the lost and the hidden
And preserve it for thy children.

QUESTIONS

1. In 1938, some skydancers came to South Bend to perform. What is a skydancer?

2. When was the worst hailstorm in South Bend history?

3. Name the Notre Dame football player who came back from being wounded in the Vietnam War to star in the NFL.

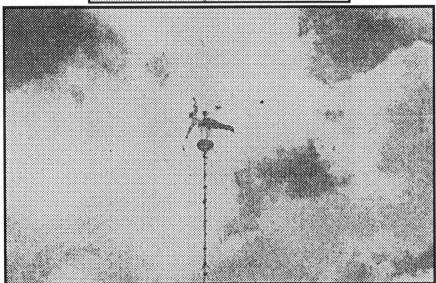

Courtesy of the South Bend Tribune

Skydancers

ANSWERS

1. In a gusty 30 MPH wind, a brother and sister team danced the Jitterbug, Suzy-Q, Big Apple, and Fox Trot on top of a tiny platform 200 feet above the Oliver Hotel. Benny Fox also stood on his hands and danced the Big Apple upside down attracting tens of thousands spectators.

South Bend News Times 8/10/1938

2. September 22, 1886 was the worst hailstorm ever known in this vicinity. The ground was white with hailstones, ranging from the size of walnut to that of a hen's egg. Some were picked up that measured an astonishing eleven inches in circumference. Window glass was broken in many homes, stores and factories and the hour hand was knocked off the Courthouse clock. Over 12,000 window lights were destroyed in the Studebaker plant alone. Notre Dame suffered a tremendous loss with many of their beautiful stained glass windows being utterly ruined.

South Bend Tribune 3/4/1922

3. Running back, Rocky Bleier, played for Notre Dame in the mid 60's, was a member of the national championship team in 1966 and served as captain in 1967. After being drafted in the sixteenth round by the Pittsburgh Steelers, he shocked the scouts by actually making the team.

Unfortunately, he was then drafted again, this time by the U.S. Army. By November of '68 he was a private and by the next June he was carrying a grenade launcher in Vietnam. On August 20, 1969, after being shot twice in the left thigh and while retreating to a safer position, he was severely injured by a grenade exploding at his feet. Surgeons in Da Nang removed most of the hundred sulfer-coated pieces of shrapnel imbedded in his legs and warned him that he'd never play football again. After his recuperation, which lasted almost two years, he earned a starting position with the Pittsburgh Steelers and became a star in the NFL. He helped the team to an unprecedented four Super Bowl victories and retired after his twelfth season. In 1980 a TV-movie called "Fighting Back" was made about his gutsy comeback starring Robert Urich as Rocky and Art Carney as team owner, Art Rooney, Sr.

Notre Dame Program 11/17/1990; Fighting Back

QUESTIONS

4. Hi, Mom! Since mothers are so special to their children, they have been honored throughout history and in many different ways. In 1914, the second Sunday in May was officially declared Mother's Day by Congress. Which local resident was called the "Father of Mother's Day"?

5. An attorney and his seven friends stood up for what they believed and it cost them $2,856, a huge sum in 1849. Some of them were forced to sell real estate holdings in order to satisfy the judgement. Do you know why they had to pay?

ANSWERS

4. Frank Hering was called the "Father of Mother's Day" because he gave the first public speech asking that a special day be set aside to honor all mothers. This South Bend resident, who was twice elected national president of the Fraternal Order of Eagles, first mentioned Mother's Day at an Eagles meeting in 1904. Hering was a professor at Notre Dame and also served as its first paid athletic director and football coach.

South Bend Tribune 7/23/1993

5. The United States Supreme Court ruled that they had to pay a Kentucky farmer for freeing his slaves in South Bend's famous Fugitive Slave Case.

Kentuckian John Norris owned a family of slaves who disappeared on October 9, 1847. Two years later Norris discovered that David and Lucy Powell and their four children were living in Cassopolis, Michigan. He went to get them back and forced those at home, Mrs. Powell and three of the children, into a covered wagon, tied them up and headed south.

Word soon spread of the abduction. A neighbor followed their tracks and after finding the Norris party near South Bend, consulted an attorney there named E. B. Crocker. They filed a writ claiming the four Powells had been kidnapped. Along with thirty or forty South Bend residents, a deputy sheriff forced Norris to release the Powells. Instead of being freed, though, Mrs. Powell and her three children were put in jail while the case was being heard.

On Friday, September 28, 1849, Judge Elisha Egbert ruled that Norris had not obtained a proper certificate before recapturing his slaves and ordered them to be set free. In a heated confrontation, Norris and his men drew their guns and threatened to shoot anyone who tried to free the Powells. Eventually, calm was returned to the courtroom but the Powells were returned to jail. Charges and counter-charges were filed and were to be decided upon the following Monday. Over the weekend more than 75 of the Powell's neighbors arrived from Cassopolis, many of them with guns. The judge again ruled in favor of the Powells and they were finally set free. This time, accompanied by their neighbors and friends, they made their way back to their home in Cassopolis.

Three months later, Norris filed suit for damages against attorney Crocker and seven other prominent citizens claiming that they knowingly helped the four Powells escape from him. The United States Supreme Court reversed the South Bend court's decision and ordered the eight men to pay Norris a total of $2,856 for his loss which included $500 for Mrs. Powell and $2250 for the children.

South Bend Tribune 3/30/1969

Courtesy of the Northern Indiana Historical Society

The Oliver Hotel

QUESTIONS

6. Who was named the "King of Stop and Go"?

7. McDonald's serves lots of hamburgers to lots of people but did you know that in 1922 there was an establishment in South Bend that served over half a million diners. That's an average of 1,400 people each day. What was the name of this place?

8. Who holds the all time Irish football record for the most rushing yards per attempt in a single season?

9. The Pinkerton national detective agency was called in on the case. They distributed reward posters across the country and enlisted hundreds of policemen and detectives in the manhunt. But even after all their work, it was a spurned woman who broke the case wide open. Four years after the crime, a Chicago prostitute identified three men as the perpetrators of the crime: her husband, who had left her for another woman; her husband's friend, a gambler and habitual criminal; and a stuttering former South Bend bartender. What was this famous local crime?

Henry Muessel

Courtesy of the Northern Indiana Historical Society

The Muessell Brewery

ANSWERS

6. Vincent Bendix, because his first two major products were automobile starters and brakes.

St. Joseph Valley Record, Fall 1990

7. The Oliver Hotel served more than one half million meals in 1922.

<u>*South Bend World Famed*</u>

8. George Gipp carried the football for an average of 8.1 yards per carry in 1920. Assuming a minimum of 100 carries per season, that record has never been broken in nearly 80 years. Reggie Brooks almost broke the record in 1992 when he averaged 8.04 yards per carry.

9. On December 30, 1915, a robbery by three men at the Muessel Brewery resulted in the deaths of two. Henry Muessel, who had just stopped in at the brewery to use the phone and chat with his cousins, and Frank Chrobet, who was the last driver to check in at the cashier's window in the brewery office, were shot and killed during a robbery which netted under $100. William Muessel, the company's bookkeeper, was shot in the stomach and, although very seriously injured, he recovered.

After the robbery, the three thieves hid just 150' from the police station and managed to slip out of town. Gus Schultz, the informant's husband, was arrested in South Bend in March 1920, found guilty of second-degree murder, and served 22 years in prison. Jack Wright was captured in Detroit in September 1920, was found guilty of first-degree murder and sentenced to life imprisonment. The third man, ex-bartender Charles Danruther, was never located.

South Bend Tribune 5/6/1990

QUESTIONS

10. On October 16, 1961, thirty-eight people were arrested at nineteen different business establishments. Arrests were made at thirteen grocery stores, three drug stores, a fruit market, a trailer rental company and an appliance store. The largest number of arrests, six, occurred at J. E. Walz, Inc. on South Michigan Street. In most cases, the arrested persons were allowed to drive in their own cars to the police station for booking. Why were all these people arrested?

11. Northern Indiana is not well known for its mines or minerals, however one mineral was found in enough quantity to warrant the creation of an industry that lasted until supplies ran out twenty years later. What was it?

12. There were Bendix automotive and aviation parts, Bendix outboard motors, and Bendix electric fans but perhaps the most well-known product that bore the Bendix name was the Bendix washing machine. When did Vincent Bendix develop the Bendix automatic washer?

ANSWERS

10. They had opened their stores on Sunday. Strict enforcement of the state's 1905 'blue laws' had begun. Stores were not allowed to do business on Sunday and those that did could expect fines ranging from $1.00 to $10.00. Most of the merchants were forced to close while they and their employees drove to the police station for booking, but they reopened their businesses as soon as they were finished. They were not re-arrested.

South Bend Tribune 10/16/1961

11. Bog iron ore. In the 1830's, there was enough iron ore in the marshes adjacent to Mishawaka that the St. Joseph County Iron Works became the principal industry in Mishawaka. Castings were made from this ore for twenty years until the supply of ore failed.

When James Oliver was sixteen, he worked at the blast furnace and foundry and in 1838, he molded an iron boot scraper. He was so proud of his first effort that he kept it. After his death, it was donated to the Northern Indiana Historical Museum.

South Bend Tribune 10/15/1933

12. He didn't. The first automatic washing machine was developed by two young inventors who worked at one of Bendix's subsidiaries. For 25% of their stock, Bendix allowed them to use his facilities to test and develop this new and unique machine and to use the Bendix name on their product. Bendix Home Appliances was founded in 1936 and at one time had 52% of the market for automatic washers. Bendix sold his shares just before WWII in order to raise cash to offset losses caused by shortages of materials.

St. Joseph Valley Record, Fall 1990

Courtesy of the Northern Indiana Historical Society

Hon. William G. George

QUESTIONS

13. Hon. William G. George was the first mayor of South Bend. He was elected in 1865 and apparently served three consecutive one-year terms. How many votes were cast in this election?

14. Three Notre Dame basketball players earned spots on the United States Olympic basketball team. Name them.

15. What was the very first automobile driven in South Bend?

16. What was behind the biggest building boom in St. Joseph County history? In St. Joseph County alone (not including the cities of South Bend or Mishawaka), 911 new homes were built at an average cost of $3,400.

17. Everyone knows what it takes to mail a letter in the U. S. today. After writing to your friend, you address the envelope being sure to include the proper zip code. Then, if it weighs less than an ounce, you affix a 33 cent stamp to it no matter where it's going, near or far. What did it take to send or receive a letter in 1829 in South Bend?

ANSWERS

13. Only 542 votes were cast in 1865. At the time, it was estimated that South Bend had a population of about 4,000 residents. South Bend was incorporated as a town in this election and immediately after that vote, George was elected mayor on the Republican ticket.

South Bend Tribune 11/9/1922

14. Vince Boryla in 1948, Adrian Dantley in 1976 and Bill Hanzlik in 1980.

Notre Dame Program 9/13/1990

15. It was a W. W. Steamobile with a 4 1/2 HP engine. Once it was fired up for a trip, this automobile took the dirt roads at 20-25 miles per hour.

South Bend Tribune 8/11/1948

16. Because of the low cost, you should have been able to guess that the reason for the building boom in 1946 was the enormous demand for housing by veterans returning from WWII. Surprisingly though, 1987 came in second with 821 new single-family dwellings totaling $3.1 million in value. That means that the price of the average new home in 1987 had gone up to $96,500.

South Bend Tribune 1/17/1988

17. Once a week, the mail carrier arrived on horseback at the log cabin general store and post office. The combination storekeeper and postmaster, Lathrop M. Taylor, unlocked the small cabinet in the corner and sorted the mail into small cubbyholes. Letters were not in envelopes; they were folded over and often sealed with wax and had no postage stamps on them. Instead, each person receiving the mail paid the postage due which was determined by its weight and the distance it traveled. There was no free mail delivery; you had to pick your mail up at the general store. The fees ranged from 1/2 cent for a letter to 59 1/2 cents for a bundle of newspapers. In 1829, the South Bend Post Office recorded quarterly proceeds of $28.33, $79.94 1/2, and $113.05. Free mail delivery did not begin until 1882.

South Bend Tribune 3/13/1949

QUESTIONS

18. Which team played Notre Dame for the first time in football?

19. Has South Bend ever had a national spelling bee champion?

Courtesy of the South Bend Tribune
Betty Robinson with Mayor Chester R. Montgomery

20. Which American president-elect always did what his wife said.....according to his wife during a South Bend campaign visit?

ANSWERS

18. Michigan University played Notre Dame on November 23, 1887. Michigan won that game, 8-0, and also won the next seven games they played. Notre Dame beat them for the first time (11-3) in 1909. After that game they didn't play each other until 1942 and 1943, when they each won one game. It was another 35 years before they played again in 1978.

Notre Dame Program 10/13/1990

19. Sure! In 1928, Betty Robinson triumphantly returned from Washington, D.C. as national elementary school spelling bee champion. A large group of city and school officials, including Mayor Chester R. Montgomery, greeted the thirteen-year-old St. Joseph parochial school student. She first arrived in Plymouth by train and then continued the trip to South Bend enthroned in a bright red Studebaker touring car. The police motorcade was greeted by the South Bend High School band and thousands of well-wishers. She received many gifts from local merchants including a diamond ring, a walnut spinet desk, a string of pearls and a diamond studded wristwatch.

South Bend Tribune 5/28/1928

20. Dwight D. Eisenhower. In September of 1952, Mamie Eisenhower, when asked how she managed to keep Ike on a correct diet during campaign trips, replied, "Ike always does what I say. He has always eaten whatever food is put before him. He was brought up that way. And I always see to it that it is the right food for him." It's as simple as that for Mamie. She even says it isn't at all difficult to keep him "in line" because he "just obeys, that's all there is to it."

South Bend Tribune 9/16/1952

QUESTIONS

21. In 1991 Sports Illustrated magazine ranked the best fifty college quarterbacks in football history. Steve Young from Brigham Young University (1981-83) placed first; Doug Flutie from Boston College (1981-84) was 15th; Joe Namath from Alabama (1962-64) was in a three-way tie for 25th; and Roger Staubach from Navy (1962-64), ranked 37th. Where did Notre Dame's best quarterbacks place?

22. What was the population of South Bend in 1835?

23. The first automobile manufactured in South Bend was an electrically powered Studebaker that held a storage battery capable of running for 50 miles. Its average speed was eleven m.p.h. on tires made of steel. After being driven through South Bend's business district, plans were made to take it to Chicago to be driven on the streets there. Thomas Edison was expected to arrive soon to consult with the Studebakers about a new storage battery he was developing. When did all this occur?

24. Have you ever heard the saying that "it rained cats and dogs"? Although no cats or dogs fell from the sky, what did come down during a rainfall in July 1937?

ANSWERS

21. John Huarte (1962-64) and Joe Theismann (1968-70) tied for 13th place. Johnny Lujack (1943 and 1946-47) placed 22nd; Joe Montana (1975-78) was ranked 31st; and Paul Hornung (1954-56) was 45th.

Sports Illustrated Classic,
Special Issue: A Celebration of Yesterday's Heroes, Fall 1991 © Time Inc.

22. The population in 1835 was 175, two-thirds of whom were men. Thirty to forty men boarded at Squire Johnson's Tavern which was a one story frame building 18' by 36'. There was a schoolhouse in town that was also used as the church. It stood only four logs high and a man couldn't stand in it with his hat on.

South Bend Times 1/9/1903

23. November 16, 1901. Through the next decade, until production ceased in 1912, the Studebaker company produced more than 1,800 electrically powered cars and trucks.

South Bend Tribune 11/16/1901

24. Hundreds of fish fell from the sky in a heavy rainstorm on the northwest side of South Bend. This phenomenon was attributed to rainspouts that lifted the small fish high into the air, carrying them many miles before dropping them back to earth in South Bend.

South Bend Tribune 7/15/1937

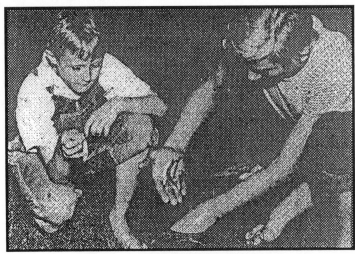

Courtesy of the South Bend Tribune
Flying Fish

QUESTIONS

25. One of Notre Dame's football captains was named an "All-American" at two different schools. Who was he?

26. Of the 25 car manufacturers at the second annual Auto Show held in South Bend in 1929, how many are still in business?

27. To what lengths did Babe Voorde go in order to ride with a Presidential candidate?

28. Why were assembly lines set up in the four public high schools and the YMCA in 1942?

Courtesy of the South Bend Tribune

Assembly Lines

ANSWERS

25. George Connor was an All-American football player at Holy Cross in 1942 and at Notre Dame in 1946 and 1947.

Notre Dame Program 10/13/1990

26. In 1929 the Granada Theater building was filled with cars made by the following manufacturers: Buick, Cadillac, Chevrolet, Chrysler, DeSoto, Dodge, Erskine, Essex, Ford, Franklin, Graham-Paige, Hudson, Hupmobile, LaSalle, Lincoln, Nash, Oakland, Oldsmobile, Pierce-Arrow, Plymouth, Pontiac, Reo, Studebaker, Willys-Knight, and Whippet. The Auto Show had over 16,000 in attendance each paying the twenty-five-cent admission fee. Of those manufacturers, only nine brands are still made: Buick, Cadillac, Chevrolet, Dodge, Ford, Lincoln, Oldsmobile, Plymouth, and Pontiac.

South Bend Tribune 2/24/1929

27. In October 1952, Adlai Stevenson arrived in South Bend where he was to be in a parade with Babe Voorde. Voorde was to have boarded the train in Chicago at 7:00 a.m. but his $2.00 tip to an elevator boy failed to produce a 5:45 a.m. wake-up call. Waking up only twenty minutes before the train's departure, not surprisingly, he missed it.

Using initiative, he hailed a cab and sped to Meigs Field where he chartered a plane to fly him to South Bend. After landing at Notre Dame, he found he had just missed the motorcade to downtown. Stranded again but not giving up, he flew to Elkhart where the plane landed in an unattended airfield. He got back into the plane for another flight, this time to the Elkhart Airport.

He was able to get a cab ride to the Elkhart train station where he arrived just as the train with Adlai Stevenson was arriving from South Bend. He boarded it and traveled with the Stevenson party to Toledo, Ohio where he finally got to ride in a parade with the Presidential candidate.

South Bend Tribune 10/23/1952

28. South Bend agreed to build 2,500 model airplanes out of the 500,000 needed nationwide. These model planes would be used to train U.S. military personnel and civilians in aircraft recognition and identification.

South Bend Tribune 2/6/1942, 2/22/1942, 2/27/1942, 9/18/1942

QUESTIONS

29. What award did the citizens of South Bend receive from Time Magazine and why?

30. Notre Dame has had five coaches inducted into the College Football Hall of Fame. Who are they?

31. Who was Leopold Pokagon?

Courtesy of the Northern Indiana Historical Society

Leopold Pokagon

ANSWERS

29. In 1960 Time Magazine's first Community Service Award honored South Bend residents for their support of the local economy and the Studebaker-Packard Corporation. The citation noted South Bend's "vision, determination and work on behalf of an industry vital to the community". There was a two-day celebration called "Time For a Lark" which included a testimonial dinner and parade. Over 70,000 residents lined the parade route to watch the Lark automobiles, floats, and bands. Studebaker closed its doors a little over three years later.

South Bend Tribune 9/7/1960, 9/27-28/1960

30. Knute Rockne (inducted in 1951), Frank Leahy (1970), Jesse Harper (1971), Ara Parseghian (1980), and Dan Devine (1985).

Notre Dame Program 9/9/1991

31. Leopold Pokagon was a chief in the Potowatomie Indian tribe for 42 years. Born a Chippewa, he was captured and made a slave to the chief of the Potowatomie. In 1833 Chief Pokagon sold the government a million acres of land surrounding the head of Lake Michigan including the site of the city of Chicago for three cents an acre. He died July 8, 1841 at the age of 66.

The Pokagons

QUESTIONS

32. Something very exciting happened on March 23, 1957 causing 75,000 people to throng the parade route in downtown South Bend. What a celebration it was! Merchants flew their American flags. There were bands, fire trucks, motorcycles and sirens. What caused all this excitement?

33. What were some of the pressing needs in South Bend as listed at the turn of the century on January 1, 1900?

ANSWERS

32. The South Bend Central High School basketball team won its second state title by defeating defending champion, Indianapolis Crispus Attucks, by a score of 67-55. The Bears had a 30-0 record, only the second school in Indiana history to finish their season with no losses. South Bend Central's John Coalman was named Mr. Basketball. Just the year before, in 1956, Crispus Attucks, led by Mr. Basketball, Oscar Robertson, became the first school to be undefeated all season.

The Bears had also won the title in 1953 to cap off Elmer McCall's first year as coach. They first defeated tiny Milan with junior Bobby Plump, 56-37, in the semifinals and then later that same day, Terre Haute's Gerstmeyer Tech 42-41. Central's Paul Harvey and Jack Quiggle joined Plump on the All-Star Team. The only other time the Bears had been to the finals was when they lost to Wingate in 1913, 15-14.

In 1954, Milan made Hoosier history by beating Gerstmeyer and then Muncie Central on a last second shot by Bobby Plump.

South Bend Tribune 3/22/1953, 3/21/1954, 3/24-25/1957

33. The more things change, the more they stay the same:

1. "Safety gates at more of the railway grade crossings.

2. Better attention to duty on the part of the Police Department.

3. A union railway station.

4. Absolutely no politics in the Police and Fire Departments.

5. Less number of lawyers in the shyster variety.

6. Less of those actions which lead to a suspicion that there is graft in the distribution of certain city contracts.

7. Less indulgence in gambling and more attention to driving it from the city."

South Bend Tribune 1/1/1900

QUESTIONS

34. How big was the largest Studebaker ever built?

From the collection of Studebaker National Museum, South Bend, Indiana

Largest Studebaker

35. Name the Notre Dame quarterback who was known as the "Springfield Rifle".

36. Billy Sunday was a nationally known evangelist in the early 1900's. He spent seven weeks in St. Joseph County during May and June of 1913. During that time he showed 6,398 people the road to salvation. Leaving on the train for his home in Winona, he tucked $10,500 into his pocket and waved good-bye to the hundreds who were there to see him off. The day before he left, he preached at three services. How many people attended?

ANSWERS

34. A gargantuan model of the Studebaker Land Cruiser was built for Chicago's 1934 Century of Progress. It was 80 feet long, 28 feet high, and 30 feet wide with a steering wheel 7 1/2 feet in diameter, tires 12 1/2 feet high and running boards 21 feet long and 5 feet wide. The doors were 14 feet wide and tall enough for an elephant to walk through without stooping. This "Studebaker" housed a small auditorium seating 80 people and was used for lectures and films. It was demolished when the fair closed. There was only one other car that approached this one in size and it was a Studebaker President convertible coupe that was exhibited at the Studebaker (later Bendix) Proving Ground. It was 21 feet long and 13 feet high. This car was used for the filming of "Wild Flowers" and was destroyed in 1936.

South Bend News Times 4/8/1934; South Bend Tribune 5/17/1936

35. Angelo Bertelli, Heisman Trophy winner in 1943.

Notre Dame Program 10/13/1990

36. It was estimated that between 32,000 and 33,000 attended. Eleven thousand packed the tabernacle in the morning, 9,000 men were there in the afternoon, and 12,000 filled every available space in the big building and stood four to five deep on the St. Joseph riverbank in the evening. Additionally, 1,500 women were present at two meetings in the afternoon. Those numbers rival some of today's TV preachers!

South Bend Tribune 6/16/1913

QUESTIONS

37. What was the largest contract ever awarded by the United States Army?

38. After their marriage on June 16,1839, Peter and Mariah Coleman became the first black family to settle in South Bend. What was his occupation?

39. Only two of Notre Dame's football opponents have winning records for games played in Notre Dame's Stadium. Can you name them?

ANSWERS

37. It was a $1.2 billion contract awarded to AM General to produce 54,000 vehicles. Nicknamed the Hummer, this "High Mobility Multi-Purpose Wheeled Vehicle" is a redesigned version of the Jeep which had been the mainstay of the Army since WWII.

South Bend Tribune 1/1/1984

38. Peter Coleman first advertised his services as a Horse Farrier (horse doctor) in the South Bend Free Press on March 14, 1840 although he had been working at least since 1839. The ad stated that "From his experience in his profession, he is enabled to treat, effectually, most of the diseases which horse 'flesh is heir to.'" This Virginia native married Mariah White on June 16, 1839 with Justice of the Peace, Francis R. Tutt, officiating. The other 'free colored man' listed in the 1840 census was Joseph Huffman, a barber. He ran an ad on February 8, 1840 stating: "Joseph Huffman, barber master of the 7th district of the State of Indiana, takes pleasure in informing the bearded community of all sexes and denominations, that he has established a Tonsoronical Bureau on the south side of Washington, nearly opposite Mr. Vail's clothing store in South Bend..."

South Bend Tribune 3/30/1969; St. Joseph County's Black Pioneers: A Survey

39. Missouri (2-0) and Clemson (1-0) are the only football teams with a winning record against Notre Dame in the Stadium.

Notre Dame Program 11/17/1990

From the collection of Studebaker National Museum, South Bend, Indiana

Car encased in ice

QUESTIONS

40. A 1933 ad appeared saying: "*WANTED* - Attractive young girl who will permit herself to be frozen in cake of ice. Write age, height and weight. Box 5, Tribune." What appeared at the corner of Michigan and Washington soon after?

41. What abruptly ended what had been the first pleasant, sunny Sunday of spring in 1965?

42. What happened when the managers of a local theater in Rochester prohibited a group of boys from congregating in the entrance?

ANSWERS

40. In a publicity stunt created by the Studebaker Corporation, a strange looking "iceberg" was towed downtown. A young lady was seated inside a 1934 Studebaker Dictator automobile that was totally surrounded by 4,000 pounds of ice at least a foot thick. She had entered the car by climbing up through the wooden floorboards.

A group of volunteers chipped away at the ice on the windshield and radiator and as soon as they were clear, the young lady started the car and drove it down the street. She had entered the car at 8:00 AM and it wasn't until noon that the police rescue squads had chipped away enough ice for her to get out.

South Bend Tribune 10/25/1933

41. On Palm Sunday, April 11, 1965, the deadliest tornado in the state's history ripped through northern Indiana leaving over 80 dead and nearly a thousand injured. Hardest hit by the twisters was Elkhart County where just under 50 people were killed. Most of the deaths occurred in a subdivision near Dunlap where numerous houses were torn apart and a trailer camp where nearly 90 mobile homes were leveled. President Lyndon Johnson came to view the devastation.

South Bend Tribune 4/12/1965

42. The boys smeared the walls outside the theater with Limburger cheese. The audience was forced to leave before the 1905 performance of "The Little Outcast" was finished because the cheese's nauseating smell permeated the theater.

South Bend Tribune 9/19/1905

Courtesy of the South Bend Tribune

Palm Sunday Tornado destruction

Courtesy of the South Bend Tribune

President Johnson views devastation

QUESTIONS

43. Over 50,000 War Bond buyers crowded into the Notre Dame Stadium in May 1945 under dark and threatening clouds. Luckily the clouds dispersed just in time for the gala show which began with the Central High School Band parading into the stadium and ending with a rousing rendition of "God Bless America". Who were the star performers appearing at this gala?

44. Vincent Bendix invented a new method of starting cars which soon replaced having to hand-crank the engine. In what year did he develop the electric starter?

45. Bargains! Shoppers today are always looking for bargains and sales are very common. But bargains and sales are not a modern innovation. In 1922, shortly after dawn, the crowds began arriving to await the opening of the stores. So many people showed up that the stores had to lock their doors allowing only 100 customers in at a time and requiring them to leave by the back door. The Winey Store was the first to give away ten new "Peace Dollars" during the morning. What was this annual event?

46. Can you name the baseball pitcher who won the most games in his Notre Dame career?

47. One of the reasons South Bend became well known was because these two companies plastered the city's name on their products. What were the names of these two companies?

Courtesy of the Northern Indiana Historical Society

South Bend Bait Company

Courtesy of the Northern Indiana Historical Society

South Bend Watch Company

ANSWERS

43. Bob Hope, Bing Crosby, Frances Langford, Jerry Colonna, Tony Romano, Vera Vague, and Skinnay Ennis and his Band.

South Bend Tribune 5/24/1945

44. Vincent Bendix developed an electric starter in 1910 but it wasn't until 1914 that the innovative starter was mass-produced. Chevrolet's "Baby Grand" was the first car built with a Bendix starter drive; over 5,500 starters were produced that first year. By 1932 over 90% of cars on the road used his starter and by then more than 35 million had been produced.

St. Joseph Valley Record, Fall 1990

45. Mishawaka was hosting its ninth annual "Dollar Days".

South Bend Tribune 5/10/1922

46. Tom Price had 40 wins from 1991-1994 which set a record for most career wins.

Notre Dame Sports Information 5/1999

47. South Bend Watch was a company that had sold nearly a million watches by 1922 in more that 10,000 retail outlets. Their slogan was "The Watch with a Purple Ribbon". By 1922, South Bend Bait was shipping millions of boxes of bait each year to domestic and foreign markets with each box prominantly displaying the city's name.

South Bend World Famed

QUESTIONS

48. Who was South Bend's first champion and for what event?

49. Whatever happened to the Palace Theater?

Courtesy of the Northern Indiana Historical Society
The Palace Theater

ANSWERS

48. In 1837, when women's achievements were barely noticed, a fourteen-year-old girl named Mary Ann Massey became the spelling champion at Bertrand, a bustling town of 1,000. This South Bend girl earned the money for a new dress, took the steamer "Davy Crockett" to Bertrand, and then won the spelling contest there. Much to her surprise, when she returned to South Bend, the whole town turned out to cheer her success.

Story of South Bend

49. Just days from its scheduled demolition in September 1959, the Palace Theater was purchased by the E. M. Morris family and immediately donated to the people of South Bend. Originally built as a combination vaudeville and movie theater with 2,700 seats, the Palace held its grand opening on November 2, 1922. With the demise of vaudeville, it became strictly a movie theater until July 7, 1959 with the last showing of "The World, the Flesh, and the Devil" starring Harry Belafonte, Inger Stevens, and Mel Ferrer.

Renamed the Morris Municipal Auditorium, it reopened on October 29, 1959 with a Broadway Theater League presentation of Joan Blondell in "The Dark at the Top of the Stairs". The 72-year old Palace Theater remains standing today as the Morris Civic Auditorium.

South Bend Tribune 11/2/1922, 7/7/1959, 9/15/1959, 11/6/1959

QUESTIONS

50. This Irish sports legend was Notre Dame's first National Football Foundation Hall of Fame pick. Who was he?

51. In 1951 the Singer plant was 100 years old. This cabinet making plant was built in South Bend because of the abundant hardwood from neighboring forests and water power from the St. Joseph River. How many employees did it have in 1951?

52. On August 2, 1861, 5,000 area residents gathered at the Courthouse. Why?

53. The Ku Klux Klan was first organized in 1921 but the police refused to let them meet so they faded from the scene until they successfully reorganized in 1923. The Klan held its first semi-public meeting in February announcing a vigorous campaign to control the Negroes and Roman Catholics. The South Bend Tribune and the South Bend News blasted the Klan and threatened to publish the names of the Klan members. The fear of this publicity was said to have slowed the local Klan membership drives. What was the Klan membership in the early twenties?

ANSWERS

50. George Gipp was chosen in 1951, the first year inductions were made into the College Football Hall of Fame. Knute Rockne and Elmer Layden were also chosen that year. George Gipp was a consensus first team All-American running back in 1920; Gus Dorais was Notre Dame's first consensus All-American at quarterback in 1913.

Notre Dame Program 9/29/1990

51. Singer had 2,000 employees. At that time, it was using one and a half million feet of imported wood and five million feet of processed wood each year. The veneering department alone used 430,000 pounds of glue.

South Bend Tribune 11/16/1951

52. Funeral services were being held for John Auten, the first soldier from Indiana to be killed by the Confederates in the Civil War. He was killed while on a scouting expedition at Laurel Hill. Three rounds of eight guns were fired over his grave during the military funeral.

St. Joseph Valley Register 7/18/1861, 8/8/1861

53. The local Klan membership was said to be from 600 to 800. The Klan continued to be active, hosting a tri-state festival and parade in 1924. Riots between Klansmen and anti-Klansmen (mostly Notre Dame students) ensued. By 1926 interest in the Klan declined so much that the local charter was withdrawn.

South Bend Remembers

QUESTIONS

54. What year did the Studebaker Corporation stop making horse-drawn carriages?

55. Everyone knows that Notre Dame is a football powerhouse and has won more national championships than any other school. How many has it won?

56. How old are the oldest animal remains found in this area?

57. Bank robberies seemed to be fairly common events in the 20's and 30's especially in the Chicago area. However, on Saturday, June 30, 1934 South Bend was the target of bandits who stole more than $28,000 and escaped after killing one man and wounding a half dozen more. The only clue left behind was a bloodstained and bullet-riddled Hudson sedan. One of the country's most famous gangsters was identified as the leader. Who was he?

ANSWERS

54. Studebaker stopped making horsedrawn carriages in 1920.

The Emergence of a City, South Bend 1920-1930

55. Since the Associated Press began naming the winner of the national championship in 1936, Notre Dame has won eight titles (1943, 1946, 1947, 1949, 1966, 1973, 1977, and 1988). Oklahoma is in second place with six titles. In addition to those eight years, Notre Dame is considered to have also won consensus national titles in 1924, 1929, and 1930.

Notre Dame Program 9/9/1991

56. Mastodon bones and teeth that dated from 25,000 B.C. were found on a farm near Walkerton.

South Bend Tribune 6/5/1931

57. John Dillinger led the June 1934 bank roberry.

South Bend News Times 6/30/1934

Courtesy of the South Bend Tribune

Mastodon Tusk

QUESTIONS

58. What was the first park in South Bend?

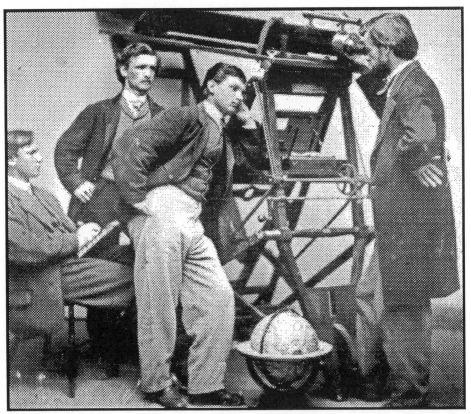

Courtesy of the Northern Indiana Historical Society
Timothy Howard with students

59. From 1922 to 1924, the "Four Horseman" lost only two games, both to the same team. Which team beat them twice?

ANSWERS

58. Howard Park was developed in 1878 followed by Leeper Park in 1895. Howard Park had been a swampy breeding ground for malaria when Timothy Howard, a city councilman, suggested that the tract be used as the town dump and later converted into a public park. The park was named after him in 1894.

Originally from Michigan, Timothy E. Howard graduated from Notre Dame in 1862 and immediately enlisted in the Twelfth Michigan Infantry to fight in the Civil War. After he was severely injured at the Battle of Shiloh, he returned to his Alma Mater to teach English and Astronomy. He became a member of the South Bend Common Council in 1878 and later studied law. He also served as South Bend's city attorney, county attorney for St. Joseph County, clerk of St. Joseph Circuit Court, state senator, and Supreme Court judge. In 1898 he became the first local man to receive Notre Dame's Laetare medal and in 1907 wrote A History of St. Joseph County. He died in 1916 at the age of 79.

History of St. Joseph County; South Bend Tribune 7/10/1916

59. Nebraska beat Notre Dame in 1922 and 1923. In 1924, Notre Dame was undefeated.

Notre Dame Program 10/13/1990

QUESTIONS

60. Have you heard the story of the bobtail cow?

61. When was the first South Bend girl chosen as Miss Indiana in the Miss America contest?

Courtesy of the South Bend Tribune

Hilda Koch, Miss Indiana

62. "Some communities have the monorail. Some have the subway. Notre Dame has the quickie." Who said this and what was the quickie?

Courtesy of the South Bend Tribune

Hilda Koch, Miss Indiana

ANSWERS

60. In 1873 Jim Studebaker and Leighton Pine had a heated discussion about what kind of water pressure system to install. When Studebaker's reservoir system was rejected, he bet Pine a cow that there would not be enough pressure from the standpipe system to drive him from the tower of his building. On Christmas Day Studebaker took his place on the tower. The Fire Department attached their hose to the fire hydrant, aimed it and knocked him off.

After Studebaker presented the cow to Pine, Pine auctioned it off with the proceeds going to the poor. The cow was sold and resold many times with it finally earning $300. As it was being led away, a butcher rushed after it with a huge knife and cut off its tail. The crowd became outraged and chased after the butcher. When he dropped the tail, the crowd realized that it had been a bobtail cow and the tail had been fastened on as a joke. The crowd dissolved into laughter and proceeded to auction off the tail. It brought an additional $45 for charity.

Story of South Bend

61. In 1927, Hilda Koch, Miss South Bend and Miss Indiana, lost to Miss Illinois in the Miss America contest. She was 19 years old, five foot two and 105 pounds with dark brown hair and blue eyes. Shelli Yoder from Shipshewana was Miss Indiana in 1992 and became second runner-up in the Miss America contest.

South Bend Tribune 9/4/1927, 2/15/1994

62. President Gerald R. Ford, on a visit to make a "major address" and receive an honorary Doctor of Laws degree from Notre Dame, made this statement. The remark, which brought the largely student audience to its feet with a roar of applause, was a reference to the shuttle bus that ran a four-mile stretch of US 31 (now SR 933) into Michigan where the 18-year old students could buy beer.

South Bend Tribune 3/17/1975

QUESTIONS

63. The Bendix Corporation made brakes for the auto industry. In 1926 they produced 650,000 brakes. What was the production two years later in 1928?

64. Shortly after the end of the Civil War, a woman with a peg leg settled near a group of Potowatomie and Cherokee Indians in the Hartford area. She purchased an eighty-acre farm and was quickly dubbed "Peg Leg Annie". Although Annie was rather short and slender, she could load a wagon with fifty-pound kegs of cider, change the iron tires on wagons, shoe horses, and was an excellent carpenter. Most of the farmers liked her because she was friendly and sociable. She was very devout and attended the church's Ladies Society meetings regularly. What made her different from the thousands of other pioneer women of her day?

65. When were evening football games first played in Notre Dame's Stadium?

66. Who was the first sheriff in St. Joseph County to be accused, tried, and convicted of a crime committed while in office?

ANSWERS

63. In 1928 Bendix produced 3,600,000 brakes, a 554% increase.

St. Joseph Valley Record, Fall 1990

64. After her death in 1904 at the age of 81, the townsfolk were shocked to learn that "Peg Leg Annie" was a man. Where he came from, what his true name was or why he chose to represent himself as a woman for nearly fifty years was never discovered. However, rumors circulated that he was involved in the Lincoln assassination plot, or that he adopted women's clothing to protect himself from the lawlessness of the gold rush in California, or that he found his wife with another man and after murdering her wore women's clothing to escape prosecution. The monument on his grave reads, Anna Storcy born January 15, 1823 died April 26, 1904.

South Bend Tribune 4/29/1904, 1/6/1985

65. In 1982, because of portable lights erected by Musco Mobile Lighting, night games could finally be played at Notre Dame.

Notre Dame Program 9/9/1991

66. In June 1981, Ralph DeMeyer was indicted by a federal grand jury of conspiracy to extort money from reputed brothel owner, Ramona Desich, in exchange for his protection. In September he was convicted and four days later, he resigned his position as St. Joseph County Sheriff. He served a three-year sentence and was fined $10,000. Released from prison on December 16, 1984 after 14 months in custody, DeMeyer was placed on federal parole. He became a free man on October 16, 1986.

South Bend Tribune 7/27/1980, 9/18/1980, 9/22/1981, 12/17/1984, 10/20/1986

QUESTIONS

67. When was the first St. Joseph County Fair held?

68. What was Notre Dame's football record in 1956, the year Paul Hornung won the Heisman Trophy?

69. Singing is universally appreciated. A special kind of singing contest was held in 1932. What was it?

70. Name the only two members of the Baseball Hall of Fame who attended Notre Dame.

ANSWERS

67. On October 11, 1841, the first fair was held in the Courthouse yard. Planning for the fair and exhibitions began in 1835. Twenty-three prizes were awarded, including: best sample of sewing silk; best ten yards of flannel, linen, and jeans; best cheese; best beet sugar; best 1/2 acre of rutabagas; best 5 acres of tame grass; and best cultivated farm. The next fair wouldn't be held until ten years later.

South Bend Tribune 3/9/1922; History of St. Joseph County

68. Notre Dame had 2 wins and 8 losses when Paul Hornung won the Heisman Trophy.

Notre Dame Program 1990

69. People weren't singing, canaries were! Weekly canary singing contests were held in Mishawaka with the bird singing the greatest number of individual notes in an hour being declared the winner. The canaries' owners tried to get their birds to sing continuously during the sixty minutes and patiently counted the individual notes. The winning canary sang 536 notes and the second place bird sang 338 notes.

South Bend Tribune 2/22/1932

Courtesy of the South Bend Tribune

Canary Singing Contest

70. Cap Anson and Carl Yastrzemski have been named to the Baseball Hall of Fame. Yastrzemski attended Notre Dame for only one semester but never actually played for the Irish.

Notre Dame Sports Information 5/1999

QUESTIONS

71. What is the significance of a chair currently displayed in the center of the Northern Indiana Historical Society Museum?

72. What was the greatest number of employees that Studebaker had and when?

73. Eighty-four year old Frank Lloyd Wright visited South Bend in May of 1953 to speak to the Indiana Society of Architects. Over 600 attended. Was there any other reason for Wright's visit?

ANSWERS

71. This high-backed chair was used by the Vice President of the United States, Schuyler Colfax, when he was the Speaker of the House of Representatives. Colfax was elected Vice President in 1866 and served under Ulysses S. Grant. The regal-looking chair has a heavily carved wooden frame bearing a shield and stars and is upholstered in a deep red tapestry.

South Bend Tribune 4/17/1949

72. Studebaker had 23,770 employees in 1923.

The Emergence of a City, South Bend 1920-1930

73. Wright wanted to see the two homes he had designed and built in South Bend. The former residence of K. C. DeRhodes, who owned the first Ford dealership, was built in 1906 at a cost of $6,000. Located at 715 West Washington, this home is Indiana's only example of Wright's prairie style of architecture from his early years. It has a light and airy feel with its 60 windows, 25 light fixtures, and tan stucco exterior. Later sold to the Avalon Grotto Club, a masonic lodge, it is now privately owned by the Thomas Miller family.

Wright's other house was commissioned by Herman and Gertrude Mossberg in 1948 at a cost of $60,000. Herman Mossberg had admired Wright's Robie House while a student at the University of Chicago so after his marriage, he asked Wright to design his new home at 1404 Ridgedale Road. Built of red brick, this imposing home resembles a fortress in the front but opens up to a Wright-designed garden in the back. In fact, in addition to the house and gardens, Wright also designed or approved all of the furnishings in the home.

There are only six Wright houses in Indiana: the two in South Bend and one each in Ft. Wayne, Marian, West Lafayette, and one along the Indiana dunes. There are also two in St. Joseph, Michigan.

South Bend Tribune 5/23-24/1953, 2/23/1954, 4/10/1994

Photos by Andy Jones

Frank Lloyd Wright Houses

QUESTIONS

74. "The citizens of our town were aroused from their slumbers at about half-past twelve o'clock, on Monday night last, by the ringing of the church bells, and on coming together, it was ascertained that, instead of a fire, an awful accident had happened but a short distance west of here..." as quoted from the Mishawaka Enterprise of Saturday, July 2, 1859. What happened?

75. What's so special about the final 22 cent commemorative stamp issued by the U. S. Postal Service?

ANSWERS

74. At the South Bend and Mishawaka border on Lincolnway East near Ironwood, a stone culvert and the embankment above it were completely washed away by heavy rains leaving a chasm thirty feet deep and one hundred feet long. A 9-car express train from Chicago was about a half-hour late for its 11:27 PM arrival into Mishawaka and was travelling at about 25-30 MPH when it approached the chasm.

The engine and tender leapt the entire distance and buried themselves totally out of sight in the opposite bank killing the engineer and fireman instantly. With the exception of the sleeping car which traveled at the end of the train, all of the cars were smashed into pieces the size of kindling wood. "The rushing of the water, the darkness of the night, and the screams and cries for help were horrid in the extreme; many were rescued while clinging to limbs of trees or other objects along the banks."

The exact number of fatalities, estimated to be between forty and seventy, was never known because some of the bodies were washed into the St. Joseph River and never found. An estimated 30 passengers were missing and 25 escaped injury. Fifteen unknown or unclaimed bodies were buried in Mishawaka, however, all but three were later claimed by the families of the victims. Over fifty passengers were injured, including a Mr. Sibley, one of the railroad's Directors.

Mishawaka Enterprise 7/2/1859, 7/9/1859, 7/16/1859

75. On March 9, 1988, Knute Rockne was honored with a stamp commemorating the hundredth anniversary of his birth. Rockne, head football coach at Notre Dame from 1918 until his death in a plane crash in 1931, was the first athletic coach to be so honored. President Ronald Reagan came to Notre Dame for the first day of issue ceremonies.

South Bend Tribune 5/14/1988

QUESTIONS

76. Dance Marathons were very popular in the Twenties. It meant dancing hour after hour with short 15-minute breaks. How long did two local contestants dance in order to win first prize?

77. One of Notre Dame's best defensive football players set the record for most fumble recoveries in his career. Who was he and how many fumbles did he recover?

78. When did rural free delivery of mail begin in South Bend?

79. South Bend Watch Company was built in 1902 on Mishawaka Avenue which at the time was a dirt road with no sidewalks or streetlights. On dark winter days, workers had to carry lanterns to and from their jobs. This immense building was 450' long by 60' wide and three stories high. The company closed in 1929 and never re-opened its doors. Associates bought the land in 1955 and planned to raze the building in September 1957. However, in July it burned to the ground. Flames and smoke shot 150 feet into the air and were visible two miles away at the fire station on Portage Avenue. South Bend Watch shipped watches all over the country and were famous for their "railroad watch". At their peak, how many watches were being produced annually?

80. Name the athlete who was coached by John Wooden, drafted by the Chicago Bears, signed by the New York Yankees, and played for the Boston Celtics.

Courtesy of the South Bend Tribune

Dance Marathoners, Theresa Popp and Darrell Morgenson

ANSWERS

76. South Bend's Darrell Morgenson and Theresa Popp began dancing on Wednesday evening, July 26, 1928 and ended 157 hours, or almost a week later, on Wednesday morning, August 1st. Thirteen couples competed in the Tokio Dance Hall for the $400 first prize. Lucky couple number 13 set the Dance Marathon record for the State of Indiana, smashing the old record of under 100 hours. The promoters promised the winners 10% of the gate receipts but disappeared without a trace right after the event. Morgenson planned to use his winnings for tuition at Notre Dame.

South Bend Tribune 7/29-8/1/1928; South Bend News Times 8/1/1928

77. Ross Browner made 12 fumble recoveries during his career as a defensive end. He was named a consensus All-American in 1976 and 1977 and received the Outland Trophy in 1976 and the Maxwell Award and the Lombardi Trophy in 1977.

Notre Dame Program 10/13/1990

78. On May 15, 1899 two carriers began delivering mail in horse-drawn carriages 53 7/8 total miles. By 1927 there were 8 carriers delivering by car a combined mileage of 242.53 miles. They not only delivered the mail, but also sold registered letters, money orders and stamps. Over seventy years later, in 1999, there are 171 postal carriers.

South Bend Tribune 5/15/1927, South Bend Post Office 5/3/1999

79. The South Bend Watch Company produced 60,000 watches a year.

South Bend Tribune 7/9/1957

80. Ed Ehlers, a successful businessman in South Bend, began his athletic career by playing basketball and baseball for Wooden at South Bend Central High School.

Sport, 8/1988

QUESTIONS

81. What did the Native Americans call the St. Joseph River?

82. The preview alone drew nearly 1,000 people to see it in 1938. What was it?

83. He was a queer looking man. For a coat, he wore a coffee sack with holes cut out for his head and arms. He sometimes wore a tin pan on his head which served double duty as a hat and a stew pan. Going barefoot most of the time, even in winter, he thought it was a sin to kill anything in order to get food. When he would visit the area, Chief Pokagon of the Potowatomie tribe would drive out to meet him in his two-wheeled wagon pulled by a team of oxen. They always had a good visit and afterwards the old chief would drive to the next village with him. He died in 1847 at the age of 72. Who was he?

84. Alex Arch, a South Bend man, was noted for a first in 1917. What was it?

85. Which famous South Bend resident was born to Swedish immigrants, Rev. John Bengtson and his wife, Anna, and, as an adult, received the title of "Knight of the North Star" from King Gustav V of Sweden?

From the collection of Studebaker National Museum, South Bend, Indiana
Vincent Bendix as a child (right)

ANSWERS

81. The "River of the Miamis of the Lakes".

History of St. Joseph County

82. Silent screen actress, Colleen Moore, brought her dollhouse to South Bend for a week long stay. It visited again for a week in 1942.

The Fairy Castle, standing seven-feet high and nine-feet square, took seven years to build at a cost of $400,000. Containing over 2,000 miniature objects including two tiny suits of armour donated by Rudolph Valentino, the intricately made fairy castle has stained glass windows, a floating staircase and a pool with running water. It can still be seen at the Museum of Science and Industry in Chicago.

South Bend Tribune 1/25/1938, 5/28/1942, 6/12/1942; Chicago 10/1991

83. John Chapman, better known as Johnny Appleseed.

The Pokagons

84. On October 22, 1917 Alex Arch was the first American to fire a shot in World War I. He used a cannon.

South Bend Tribune 9/29/1919

85. Vincent Bendix was born in 1881 in Moline, Illinois where his parents changed their family name. Bendix remained fluent in Swedish and hired many Swedish immigrants to work in his plants, often speaking to them in their native language.

St. Joseph Valley Record, Fall 1990

QUESTIONS

86. What record was set in June 1988?

87. Two thousand seems to be a magic number when it comes to Notre Dame basketball and football statistics. How many Notre Dame basketball players have scored over 2,000 points and how many Notre Dame quarterbacks have thrown for more than 2,000 yards in a season? Can you name them?

88. Moraine deposits are masses of rocks and other materials that were carried and then deposited by a glacier. How many moraine deposits are there in St. Joseph County and where are they located?

89. Which ex-Notre Dame student was a member of the exclusive Order of the Purple Garter as well as a member of the Order of the Million Elephants and the White Parasol, the highest honor Laos could bestow on a man?

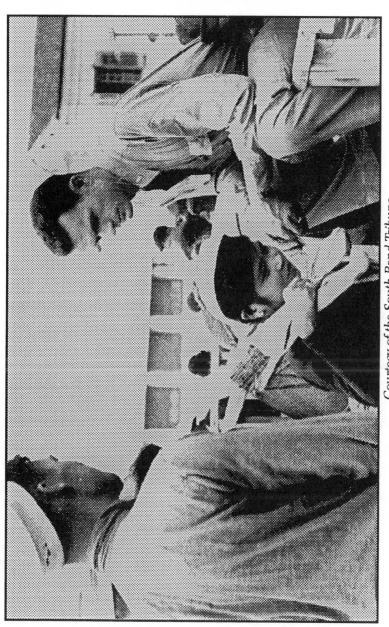

Courtesy of the South Bend Tribune

Thomas A. Dooley III

ANSWERS

86. The least amount of rainfall, 0.48 of an inch, fell in South Bend during the whole month. In fact, it barely rained in May or June either. It was the worst drought in 50 years.

South Bend Tribune 1/1/1989

87. Six basketball players have scored more than 2,000 points: Austin Carr, Adrian Dantley, David Rivers, Pat Garrity, Beth Morgan, and Katryna Gaither.

Six quarterbacks have thrown for more than 2,000 yards in a season: John Huarte, Joe Theismann, Joe Montana, Steve Beuerlein, Rick Mirer, and Ron Powlus.

Notre Dame Sports Information 5/1999

88. There are three moraine deposits. One of the highest parts of the Maxinkuckee Moraine is just south of Marian High School at Mount Alverno.

The Knollwood subdivision in Granger is part of the Kalamazoo Moraine which extends northeast across the state line into Cass County, Michigan.

Bendix Woods County Park west of South Bend is part of the Valparaiso Moraine and its series of ridges extend all the way to Lake Michigan.

South Bend Tribune 1/2/1989

89. Thomas A. Dooley III was a missionary doctor who founded two mountain hospitals in northern Laos. He attended Notre Dame but never actually graduated. He enrolled in 1944 but left while still a seventeen-year-old to enlist in the Navy. After the war he was a Notre Dame student from 1946-48 but entered St. Louis University School of Medicine before completing his undergraduate degree. He helped found MEDICO, a private organization in which doctors and nurses give a year or two of their professional lives to set up clinics in Third World countries. He was able to raise two million dollars worth of drugs and equipment and $300,000 in cash for MEDICO in less than six months. In January, 1961 he died of lung cancer at the age of 34. In addition to the Laotian awards, Tom Dooley received an honorary degree from Notre Dame in 1960 and was awarded the Congressional Medal of Honor posthumously in 1962.

South Bend Tribune, 11/15/1959, 5/10/1961; Promises to Keep

QUESTIONS

90. Who was the first white man to step foot in any part of Indiana and where?

91. After Army paid Notre Dame $1,000 to play them for the first time in 1913, the Irish traveled by train to West Point. Much to Army's surprise, Notre Dame soundly thrashed them, 35-13. The Irish took a mere 18 players to the game and only had 14 pairs of cleats. Who was sitting on the bench for Army that day.

92. In 1914 the English government placed an order that was the largest single order in its history up until that time. What did they order?

93. What local landmark measured a half-mile in circumference and stood 45 feet high in 1930?

94. Who was the first man in American political history to preside over both branches of Congress?

95. The Palace Theater opened its doors in October 1922. There were five stage acts including Carlton Emmy and his Mad Wags (acrobatic dogs), the Dufor Brothers (dancers), Dainty June & Company (child actors), Stan Stanley & Co. (comedy act), and Patsy Shelly (dancer) with Erny Holmgren and his band. They also had a screen feature, "The Cowboy and the Lady", starring Mary Miles Minter and Tom Moore. How much did it cost to get in?

ANSWERS

90. In 1679 Robert Cavelier Sieur de La Salle canoed around the southern end of Lake Michigan to the mouth of the St. Joseph River where he travelled up it to the present site of South Bend.

South Bend Tribune 8/29/1925

91. Dwight D. Eisenhower sat on Army's bench.

Notre Dame Football Media Guide

92. At the outbreak of World War I in August 1914, the English government ordered 3,000 transport wagons, 20,000 sets of harnesses and 60,000 saddles from the Studebaker Corporation.

Story of South Bend

93. It is the Notre Dame Stadium which took four months to build in 1930 at a cost of $750,000.

Notre Dame Program 9/9/1991

94. Schuyler Colfax, a representative from St. Joseph County, was Speaker of the House for 6 years from March 4, 1863 until March 3, 1869. Then he was elected Vice President of the United States and served as chief officer of the Senate for four years from March 4, 1869 until March 3, 1873.

South Bend Tribune 1/1/1989

95. Admission was 22 cents for adults and 13 cents for children under twelve.

South Bend Tribune 11/2-3/1922

Courtesy of the Northern Indiana Historical Society

Robert Cavelier Sieur de LaSalle, at the Miami Treaty, May 1681

QUESTIONS

96. During one football game in 1966, the Notre Dame students chanted, "Ara, make it stop!" Stop what?

97. Beginning with the first keel boat which was built in 1831 and the arrival of steam boats in 1832, the St. Joseph River was used for carrying freight. Why did it cease being used for this purpose?

98. Julie Krone from Eau Claire, Michigan is only 4-foot 10-inches tall and 100 pounds but she is tops in her field. What does she do for a living?

99. When was a fishing license first required for St. Joseph County residents?

100. Which famed local inventor began his career as an elevator operator in a hospital?

Courtesy of the Northern Indiana Historical Society

Vincent Bendix

ANSWERS

96. On a very rainy Saturday, the students chanted to Coach Ara Parseghian to make it stop raining. Ara turned to the crowd, raised his hands, and much to everyone's amazement, the rain stopped.

Notre Dame Program 9/9/1991

97. The St. Joseph River became increasingly difficult to navigate because of the development of dams for water power.

South Bend Tribune 8/29/1925

98. In 1987 Julie Krone became the winningest female jockey in history at the age of 24. With $13.5 million in career winnings and 1,205 victories, she was ranked sixth in the nation amongst all riders, male or female. Generally riding in nine races a day six days a week, she was the first woman to ride four winners in a single day in New York. Earlier in her career, she showed horses at local horse shows and at the Berrien County Youth Fair.

On June 5, 1993 she became the first woman jockey to win a Triple Crown race when she rode Colonial Affair to victory in the Belmont Stakes. Other women jockeys had ridden in the Kentucky Derby and the Preakness but Krone was the only woman ever to have ridden in the Belmont, winning on her third try.

South Bend Tribune 4/17/1988, 5/1/1992, 6/6/1993

99. In 1933 fishing licenses were required for everyone except persons under 18, ex-servicemen, or war nurses. The fee was $1.00 for residents and $2.25 for non-residents.

South Bend News Times 3/15/1933; South Bend Tribune 6/16/1933

100. When Vincent Bendix was 16, he got his first job as an elevator operator. He later held a string of odd jobs, picking up skills in electricity, stenography, accounting and law. During those years, he attended night school to study engineering and also raced motorcycles.

St. Joseph Valley Record, Fall 1990

QUESTIONS

101. How were the St. Joseph County Fairgrounds used during the Civil War?

102. Notre Dame's nickname, the "Fighting Irish", has been around since the late 1920's but before then, they had two other nicknames. What were they?

103. Approximately 100,000 people attended the Interstate Fair at Playland Park during its five-day run in August, 1926. Culver Military Academy's Black Horse Troop performed; daily horse races took place with a world record set on the half-mile track; and nightly fireworks lit up the sky. The biggest attraction at the fair, though, was the Medich twins. Who were they?

104. There were five major Indian trails in South Bend. Where were they located?

ANSWERS

101. The St. Joseph County Fairgrounds, which were located on seven acres of land on Portage Avenue, was used as a military camp for training and organizing troops.

South Bend Tribune 3/4/1922

102. During the 1800's, Notre Dame's athletes were known as the "Catholics". Later, during the era of the "Four Horsemen" in the early 1920's, they were called the "Ramblers". The nickname, "Fighting Irish", was officially adopted by President Matthew Walsh in 1927.

Notre Dame Program 10/6/1990

103. Nearly 40,000 people viewed South Bend's famous "linked sisters" as the babies lay behind a glass partition. Born in St. Joseph Hospital on May 22, 1926, they were joined at the chest facing each other top-to-bottom. At birth they weighed eleven pounds and measured 19 inches from the top of one head down the torso to the top of the other head. Their legs protruded from the side. Doctors said that even though they did not share a heart, they could not be surgically separated. They were on exhibition in Minneapolis when Lucy contracted pneumonia and died on October 10, 1926. Bessie died a few minutes later.

South Bend Tribune 5/24/1926, 8/8/1926, 10/10/1926

104. Portage Trail ran from the Pinhook bend of the St. Joseph River to the head waters of the Kankakee River. It is now called Portage Avenue.

Dragoon Trace was a trail followed by fur traders from Ft. Wayne to South Bend. Lincolnway East makes up part of this trail. Michigan Road, now South Michigan Avenue, led to Twin Lakes and Lake Maxinkuckee.

The two other trails are now Sumption Prairie Road to the southwest and South Bend Avenue to the northeast.

The Pokagons

QUESTIONS

105. Adlai Stevenson made a brief campaign stop in South Bend as he stumped from Chicago to Buffalo. Here for only about an hour, he made speeches at Union Station and Notre Dame. That same day he would make speeches in Elkhart and Toledo, Ohio. In the midst of this busy schedule, he took the time to do something special for thirteen-year-old Kevin Butler. What was it?

106. What company was the largest income tax contributor in the state of Indiana in 1926?

107. Between 1936 and 1993, 390 Notre Dame football players have been drafted by National Football League teams. Of those, 52 players were picked in the first round and five of them were picked first overall, more than at any other school. In which year were the most Notre Dame players drafted?

108. Telephones are an integral part of our lives today. When and where was the first telephone installed in South Bend?

109. In 1931, Vincent Bendix sponsored the first transcontinental airplane race. Who won that first Bendix Trophy Race?

ANSWERS

105. Kevin Butler, who grew up to be a prominent local attorney, had broken his leg in a parochial school football game. Adlai Stevenson autographed his cast.

South Bend Tribune 10/22/1952; the Paul Butler family

106. The Studebaker Corporation employed 22,922 workers at the time. Their profits totaled $13,042,119.

Emergence of a City, South Bend 1920-1930

107. In 1946 sixteen Notre Dame football players were drafted by the NFL including first overall pick, quarterback Frank Dancewicz, who was drafted by Boston. One of Notre Dame's other four first-round picks was Johnny Lujack who was chosen by the Bears.

Notre Dame Program 1993

108. In 1878 the first local telephone was installed with a line running from the telegraph office to the Oliver Plow Works. The first telephone exchange was established in 1880. Poles and telephone wires were erected in 1889 and the long distance telephone company extended its lines through South Bend from New York to Chicago in 1893.

The Pokagons; South Bend Tribune 1/1/1989

109. Famed pilot, Jimmy Doolittle, flying at an average speed of 223 mph from Los Angeles to Cleveland, won in 9 hours and 10 minutes. Other entrants in those early years were Amelia Earhart, Roscoe Turner and Jacqueline Cochran. Howard Hughes entered a plane in 1935 but it never ran. The last race was held in 1962 and was won by a B-58 flying 1,215 mph from Los Angeles to New York, taking 2 hours and one minute. The Bendix Trophy was retired and is now in the Smithsonian National Air and Science Museum.

St. Joseph Valley Record, Fall 1990; South Bend News Times 8/11/1935,8/29/1935

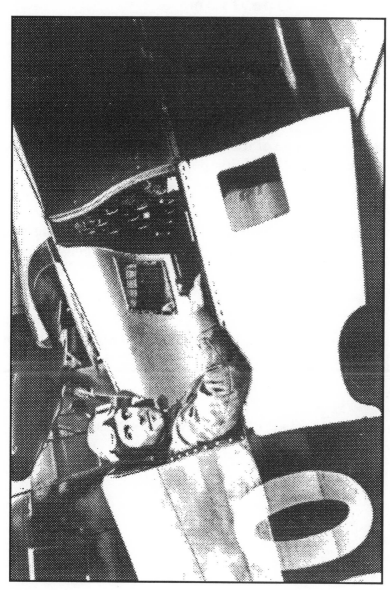

Courtesy of the Northern Indiana Historical Society

Jimmy Doolittle

QUESTIONS

110. Who caused local Kiwanians' faces to turn bright red in 1953?

111. Knute Rockne was one of the most famous football coaches at Notre Dame. What was his winning percentage?

112. In 1865, when most families had fireplaces for heating and cooking, they often became hosts to unexpected guests. Who would visit?

113. The Kankakee River in St. Joseph County is not much bigger than a ditch today. How big was it during the glacial age?

114. In the 1940's, what did the average Russian call any foreign-made automobile?

ANSWERS

110. Anita Ekberg, the 125-pound, 5-foot-7-inch blond with 37-22-36 measurements, settled herself onto the laps of several members of the Kiwanis Club causing each of them to blush. She was visiting South Bend in January, 1953 while promoting her new film, "Mississippi Gambler".

South Bend Tribune 1/23/1953

111. Knute Rockne's winning percentage of .881 remains the highest in football history at the collegiate or professional level. He coached Notre Dame to 105 victories while losing 12 and tying 5. His teams were undefeated five times and national champions six times. He was Notre Dame's head coach from 1918 until his untimely death in 1931.

Notre Dame Program 9/9/1991

112. Often, homeowners would awaken to see one or more Indian braves rolled up in their blankets with feet facing the fire, comfortably asleep. By morning, they would be gone.

The Making of a Museum

113. The glacial Kankakee River was wider and deeper than the Mississippi River. In places it was 13 miles wide and more than 100 feet deep. Tippecanoe Place stands on the sandbar that separated the Kankakee River from the St. Joseph River. Wilson Park, on the far south side of Mishawaka, is nestled in a small ancient bay of the old glacial river.

South Bend Tribune 1/2/1989

114. According to John Strohm, author of many articles and books about life in Russia, people in Russia generally referred to foreign-made motorized vehicles as "Studebakers". They told him everywhere he went that Studebaker trucks had won the war.

South Bend Tribune 10/13/1946

QUESTIONS

115. St. Joseph County and Elkhart County were created by the state legislature in 1830 and were the first counties in northern Indiana. How big were they and what was their jurisdiction?

116. What is the largest living advertising sign in the world?

117. Out of all the freshmen playing sports at Notre Dame, only four were unanimously chosen for their respective Big East All Rookie Teams in 1998-99. Can you name them?

118. Indiana had the highest turnout in the nation in the 1888 presidential election. What was the percentage of voters voting in this election?

119. What place in St Joseph County has been averaging at least 1,000 visitors per month since its opening in 1895?

ANSWERS

115. St. Joseph County was originally thirty miles square and its jurisdiction extended westward to the Illinois border. Elkhart County's jurisdiction extended eastward to the Ohio border.

South Bend Tribune 4/5/1970;
Northern Indiana Historical Society 12/1990 Calendar

116. The Studebaker tree sign, which is still growing in Bendix Woods County Park, is listed in the Guiness Book of World Records as the world's largest living advertising sign. Planted in 1938 in what used to be the proving grounds for the Studebaker Corporation, the 8,259 white pine trees spell out the name Studebaker. Each letter is currently 200 feet wide, 200 feet long and 60 feet tall.

South Bend Tribune 5/17/1988

117. Troy Murphy, Lindsey Jones, Jennifer Kriech and Jarrah Myers were unanimous picks on their respective Big East All Rookie Teams. Two of them also won Rookie of the Year honors: Troy Murphy for men's basketball and Jarrah Myers, a third baseman, for softball. Jennifer Kriech an outfielder on the softball team, also made the All Big East First Team. Lindsey Jones was one of only five unanimous picks for women's soccer. Hockey player David Inman was named to the Central Collegiate Hockey Association's All-Rookie Team and was one of three finalists for Rookie of the Year.

Notre Dame Sports Information 5/1999 (OK, OK, Lindsey is my daughter!)

118. Nearly 99 percent of registered Hoosiers cast ballots in the 1888 presidential election. Other states with a high turnout were: Kansas with 95 percent, Nebraska with 94 percent, and Minnesota with 92 percent voting.

South Bend Tribune 9/17/1989

119. The Northern Indiana Historical Society.

South Bend Tribune 4/29/1948; Northern Indiana Historical Society, 1994

From the collection of Studebaker National Museum, South Bend, Indiana

Studebaker Tree Sign in 1932

QUESTIONS

120. How large an impact did the closing of the Studebaker plant have on local unemployment figures?

121. Many South Bend residents have heard of the Council Oak but who knows why it was called that and where is it located?

Courtesy of the Northern Indiana Historical Society
Council Oak

122. Notre Dame was playing Iowa in 1955 and the score was tied with 2:15 remaining on the clock. Who kicked the winning field goal?

ANSWERS

120. The Studebaker plant closed its doors in December 1963. In October of that year, shortly before the closing, South Bend's unemployment rate was 2.4 percent. By January 1964, a month after the closing, it had risen to 8.4 percent. A year later, in December 1964, the unemployment rate was stll elevated at 5.7 percent but by the next month it had dropped back to 2.5 percent.

South Bend Tribune 12/6/1988

121. The Council Oak was an enormous oak tree, estimated to be 450 years old. The explorer, LaSalle, was said to have made many treaties with the Indians under this tree beginning with his first trip over the portage from the St. Joseph River to the Kankakee River in December of 1679. Also called the Witness Tree and the Treaty Tree, it was the site of a LaSalle treaty in May 1681 that united the Miami Indian tribes with the Potawatomies to fight against the incursions of the fierce Iroquois.

The Council Oak stood in the Highland Cemetery off of Portage Avenue until a heavy windstorm in the summer of 1991 caused it to fall. Its stump remains. Pieces of the Council Oak are for sale at the Northern Indiana Historical Society Museum.

Historic Background of South Bend and St. Joseph County in Northern Indiana

122. Paul Hornung kicked the field goal that put Notre Dame ahead of Iowa 17-14.

Notre Dame Program 1990

QUESTIONS

123. When was the South Bend's first public Christmas tree decorated?

124. There are many odd-looking vehicles on the road but one of the most unusual was travelling on South Bend's streets in 1989. What was it?

125. Which came first in South Bend, paved streets or sewers?

126. On one football trip to Penn State in 1925, the train conductor became suspicious. He locked every compartment on the train and rechecked all the tickets. Much to Knute Rockne's "surprise", the conducter discovered seven extra passengers. Who were they?

127. In 1939, they banned this in the Palais Royale. What was banned?

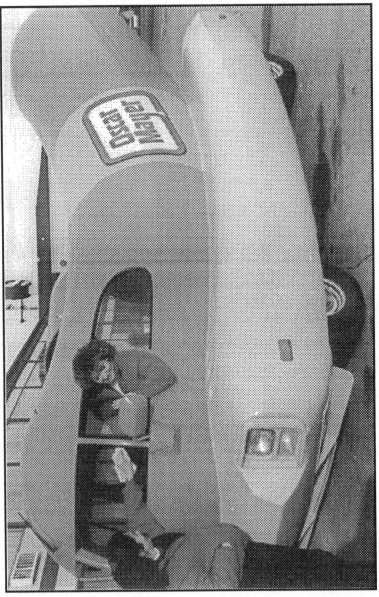

Courtesy of the South Bend Tribune

Wienermobile

ANSWERS

123. South Bend's first public Christmas tree was decorated in 1855.
South Bend Tribune 1/1/1989

124. The 23-foot-long Oscar Meyer Wienermobile spent two days driving through the area, emitting the odor of roasting hot dogs and broadcasting five different versions of the "I wish I were an Oscar Meyer Wiener" jingle. The enormous frankfurter, built on a customized Chevrolet van, was originally designed by a former Studebaker engineer, Brook Stevens.
South Bend Tribune 2/17/1989

125. Sanitation won out. Construction of sewers began in October 1861 while brick paving of streets did not begin until 1889.
Northern Indiana Historical Society Fall 1988 Calendar

126. The extra passengers on the Penn State trip were the "Notre Dame bums" also known as student managers. The stow-aways would be hidden by the players beneath their Pullman berths when travelling to away games but this time they were caught. Knute Rockne expressed shock that they were there, but he knew that somehow they turned up at all the away games.
Notre Dame Program 9/9/1991

127. Jitterbugging was banned on February 22, 1939 because the youthful "whirling dervishes" were driving the more sedate patrons away. Jitterbuggers were told that they would be escorted from the floor if they persisted in acrobatic dancing. The manager of the Palais Royale stated that "the dance floor will hold only half as many persons dancing the jitterbug steps as when more orthodox steps prevail. Consequently, income has been curtailed. There is also danger of weakening the building by wild dancing and the danger that someone will be hurt in acrobatic gyrations."
South Bend Tribune 2/22/1939

Courtesy of the Northern Indiana Historical Society

Notre Dame football players on their way to an away game.

QUESTIONS

128. When was the first marriage license issued in St. Joseph County?

129. Why were baby carriages lined up along the sidewalk in the pouring rain in May 1918?

130. According to a story told by Mrs. Frederick Elbel in *The Making of a Museum,* Yankee Harris moved to the area in the early 1800's and began to badger and blackmail residents into selling him their land. Then one night, a couple of gentlemen visited him and suggested that they go for a moonlight stroll. As they were enjoying the beauty of the riverfront scene, a group of citizens dressed up as wild Indians with tomahawks carried Yankee Harris off and did what?

131. Can you name three Notre Dame Heisman Trophy winners who also played basketball for the Irish?

132. Zimmer Corporation was founded in 1927 by a splint salesman in Warsaw who saw the need for a better product. What was his innovative idea?

ANSWERS

128. St. Joseph County's first marriage license was issued on March 29, 1834.

Northern Indiana Historical Society 3/1990 Calendar

129. May 25, 1918 was the first day of children's registration in St. Joseph County. All children under the age of six were to be weighed and measured to determine their physical condition. The objective was to discover children who did not measure up to the standard and to find out why. The ailments most prevalent among the children were adenoids ("as a result of the use of pacifiers"), infected tonsils, tubercular glands, and rickets. The pouring rain seemed to have little effect upon the turnout and, at times, the line of baby carriages extended the entire length of the block.

South Bend Tribune 5/22, 5/25, 5/30/1918

130. They gave him a suit of tar and feathers and sent him out of town.

The Making of a Museum

131. Heisman Trophy winners John Lattner, Johnny Lujack and Paul Hornung also played basketball for the Irish.

Notre Dame Program 1990

132. Up until that time, splints were being made out of papier-mache or molded wire mesh and had to be removed before x-raying the patient. Justin O. Zimmer developed an entirely new concept by making splints out of perforated aluminum. This allowed x-rays to be taken without removing the splint. They were introduced at the American Medical Association meeting in Washington D.C. that year and were immediately accepted by the medical profession.

South Bend Tribune 1/1/1989

QUESTIONS

133. This pilot was flying a Lincoln-Standard airplane from St. Louis, Missouri to Wyatt, Indiana where he was to deliver it to Jesse Grose, a flight instructor. Just after he passed Notre Dame's Golden Dome, he got lost and was forced to land and call Grose for directions. Grose drove there and flew with the pilot to Wyatt but on the way the engine started smoking. The plane made another unscheduled landing in another farmyard and this time they hauled water across the fields to fill an over-heated radiator. When they finally arrived in Wyatt, Grose checked out and soloed in the plane. Afterwards he returned the pilot to South Bend so he could catch the South Shore to Chicago where he picked up a mail plane for his return trip home. Who was the pilot?

134. It's a known fact that college students love to party especially on the weekends. But at Notre Dame, a group of fun-loving students does something far different. What is it?

135. Those areas listed as having national, state, county or local historic significance by the U.S. Department of Interior are called National Register Historic Districts. How many such districts does South Bend have listed in the National Register of Historic Places?

Courtesy of the South Bend Tribune

Charles A. Lindbergh

ANSWERS

133. Charles A. Lindbergh, who flew mail planes in St. Louis and delivered planes occasionally, delivered this plane to Wyatt. It was only 11 months later that "Lucky Lindy" flew the "Spirit of St. Louis" non-stop to Paris.

South Bend Tribune 12/9/1990

134. In the fall, before football games, over 100 Notre Dame students gather on Friday nights (Thursdays before an away game) to repaint the football team's golden helmets. Because of varying weather conditions, they use a different blend of gold dust, lacquer, and lacquer thinner each time. In dry, warm weather it can take as little as four hours to complete the job, but if it's cold and rainy, it can take all night.

Blue & Gold Illustrated, 10/28/1991

Students repainting Notre Dame football helmets

135. Three have been designated in South Bend: the West Washington National Register District, the Chapin Park National Register District (also known as the Park Avenue neighborhood), and the St. Casimir Parish Historic District, surrounding the 100-year old church. There are six local historic districts: East Wayne Street, Edgewater Place, Lincoln Way East, Riverside Drive, West North Shore, and River Bend (east of Memorial Hospital).

South Bend's Historic Districts brochure

QUESTIONS

136. LaSalle is well known as a great explorer but when he was exploring here in 1679, he managed to get lost. LaSalle and his 32 men were traveling up the St. Joseph River looking for the blazed trees which marked the portage to the Kankakee River near present-day Riverview Cemetery. Where did he end up?

Courtesy of the Northern Indiana Historical Society
Robert Cavelier Sieur de LaSalle

137. What were the coldest and hottest temperatures recorded in St. Joseph County?

138. What was the Notre Dame football team's widest margin of victory in Notre Dame Stadium?

ANSWERS

136. LaSalle and his men totally missed the specially marked trees and continued up river until they made camp across from the current IUSB campus. LaSalle left his men there while he traveled inland to find the Indian trail. He finally found it but during his search wandered through parts of Mishawaka and into Osceola. After spending the night alone in the woods, he came upon one of his men near the present-day Michigan Street bridge. By now they were searching for him because they had already found the portage thanks to their Indian guide, White Beaver. Soon all of them continued their journey west.

Eight years later, LaSalle got lost again in Texas while searching for the Mississippi River but this time one of his disgruntled men killed him.

South Bend Tribune 10/27/1991

137. On January 13, 1943 the record low temperature was minus 22 degrees. On January 20, 1985 the wind chill was minus 80 degrees which set a new wind chill record. A record high of 109 degrees was set on July 24, 1934.

WSBT Weather Calendar

138. In 1932 Notre Dame played Haskell in the Notre Dame Stadium and beat them 73-0. Notre Dame's most lopsided defeat in the stadium occurred in 1956 when they lost to Oklahoma 40-0. Their widest margin of victory anywhere took place in 1905 when Notre Dame beat American Medical 142-0 and their worst defeat was in 1944 when they lost to Army 59-0.

Notre Dame Program 9/9/1991

QUESTIONS

139. What did a banana split cost in 1933?

140. Laddie, a collie belonging to the Patterson family on South 36th Street, received the National Hero Medal from a major dog food manufacturer. What did Laddie do to deserve the medal?

Courtesy of the South Bend Tribune

Laddie with Patterson family

141. Which American president was the first to set foot in the city of South Bend while still serving in office?

ANSWERS

139. Banana splits cost 10 cents each at the Philadelphia which was located at 116 North Michigan in South Bend.

Northern Indiana Historical Society Calendar 4/1991

140. Laddie saved the life of his owner's son who was trapped under a fallen automobile. On May 9, 1957, Jack Shipley was working on a car in his father's garage when the jack collapsed. He was pinned under the car with the rear axle pressing onto his abdomen. Shipley was barely able to breathe and could not call out for help so he whispered to Laddie to "Get Mom". Laddie, realizing something was wrong, began barking and attracted the attention of neighbors who then called the police.

South Bend Tribune 6/26/1957

141. Franklin Delano Roosevelt (32nd president) arrived in South Bend on December 9, 1935 to receive an honorary LLD degree at the University of Notre Dame. A crowd estimated at 100,000 lined the processional route.

Other sitting presidents who came to South Bend were Harry Truman (33rd), Dwight Eisenhower (34th), Lyndon Johnson (36th), Gerald Ford (38th), Jimmy Carter, (39th), Ronald Reagan (40th), George Bush (41st), and Bill Clinton (42nd). Woodrow Wilson (28th) spent five minutes in South Bend in 1916 but never stepped off the train. William Howard Taft (27th) came to the city as a presidential candidate as did Rutherford B. Hayes (19th) and James Garfield (20th). When traveling through South Bend in 1880, Ulysses S. Grant (18th) made an appearance on the train platform but he was no longer president. Theodore Roosevelt (26th), Calvin Coolidge (30th), and Richard Nixon (37th) visited here while serving as Vice-President. William McKinley (25th), Warren G. Harding (29th), and John F. Kennedy (35th) travelled here while still in Congress. Benjamin Harrison (23rd) campaigned for the Senate here. Andrew Johnson (17th) who became President after Abraham Lincon's assassination, made a speech in Niles on September 5, 1866. There is no record of Herbert Hoover (31st), Grover Cleveland (22nd and 24th), or Chester Arthur (21st) ever having visited South Bend.

South Bend Tribune 9/30/1880, 12/9/1935, 10/14/1990, 3/31/1992, 5/5/1992

QUESTIONS

142. Our busy streets would be chaotic without traffic signals. When was South Bend's first traffic light installed?

143. Lou Holtz, Notre Dame's former football coach, had an excellent win-loss record (100-30-2). However, there is one man who has the best winning percentage for football games. Who in modern times has the best win-loss record?

144. Nathaniel Crum found something with a circumference of four feet, seven and three/fourths inches on July 31, 1900. What was it?

145. Mishawaka residents were having trouble with their mail service in 1916 and complained to postal authorities about it. Why wouldn't the mail go through?

146. St. Joseph County has been home to many industrial firms employing thousands of workers. Studebaker, Bendix and Ball-Band were three of the biggest. By 1993 many of those companies had moved, gone out of business or changed hands. Who was the largest employer in St. Joseph County in 1993?

ANSWERS

142. The first traffic light in the city of South Bend was installed at the corner of Main and Jefferson Streets in May 1923.

Northern Indiana Historical Society Calendar, 5/1991

143. Edward "Moose" Krause won 100% of the games he coached. Of course, he only coached two games, when Coach Leahy was in the Mayo clinic, and won them both. Considering only "true" coaches, John L. Marks has the best winning percentage (.933), then Thomas Barry (.893), Victor Place (.889) and Knute Rockne (.881) in fourth place. The coaches who had better than 80% winning records were: Jesse Harper, Frank Longman, Frank Leahy, Ara Parseghian, James Faragher, and Ed McKeever. Lou Holtz's winning percentage was 76.5%.

1998 Notre Dame Football Media Guide

144. While in the woods near Crumstown, Nathaniel Crum found a gigantic puff ball mushroom weighing ten pounds.

Northern Indiana Historical Society Calendar summer, 1991

145. Mail in those days was placed in a sack, hung on a contraption over the railroad tracks, and then scooped from the hook by a passing train. The New York Central Railroad was having trouble with its catcher service which instead of scooping the sack of mail onto the train, was ripping the pouch and sometimes cutting the mail itself. One time, when the pouch was discovered missing, they found that the mail had been thrown under the wheels of the train and was strewn along the tracks all the way to South Bend.

South Bend Tribune 10/13/1991

146. At its peak in 1923, Studebaker employed 23,770 workers. In 1993 the area's largest employer was the University of Notre Dame with 3,500 employees. Next on the list were Allied Signal Divisions (formerly Bendix), South Bend Community School Corporation, and Memorial Health Systems, each employing about 2,300 workers.

St. Joseph County at a Glance, 1993; Emergence of a City, South Bend 1920-1930

QUESTIONS

147. What unusual weather-related event occurred in August 1882?

148. In current times, boxers travel to Las Vegas or other exotic places for title fights. However, in 1920, a title fight took place in Benton Harbor, Michigan. Who defended his title there?

149. Early in the 1900's, you could buy a postcard in LaPorte County featuring a young woman saying, "Come join me in LaPorte. If you don't, I'll axe you." Do you know the story behind this gruesome card?

Courtesy of the LaPorte County Historical Society

Belle Gunness with her children.

ANSWERS

147. You guessed it! It snowed on Lake Michigan, depositing six inches of slushy snow on passing ships.

Northern Indiana Historical Society Calendar, summer, 1991.

148. Jack Dempsey fought a has-been fighter named Billy Miske on Labor Day in Benton Harbor. Over 18,000 fans watched as Dempsey knocked out Miske in the third round. Dempsey earned $ 50,000 for the match and Miske took home $ 25,000. Dempsey continued to defend his title until he lost a 10-round decision to Gene Tunney in 1926.

South Bend Tribune 2/25/1990

149. In 1901 a young widow, Belle Sorenson, bought a small farm in LaPorte after her husband and two of her young children had died unexpectedly in Chicago. She brought with her three daughters, one of whom was adopted. Two years after moving to LaPorte, she married Peter Gunness but eight months later she was widowed again when a meat grinder fell on his head. Like her first husband, Peter Gunness was insured.

Some time later, she began advertising in a Norwegian language newspaper seeking a spouse who had money or was insured. She encouraged those who responded to come to LaPorte and to bring their money with them. When they arrived, Belle had them deposit their money into her bank account for safekeeping and introduced them as her cousins or brothers. None of them stayed very long. Finally in 1908, the brother of one these men wrote Belle that he was coming to LaPorte to look for him. Just a few days before he was scheduled to arrive, Belle's home burned to the ground. Four bodies were found: the two Sorenson girls, a little boy known as Philip Gunness and the headless body of an adult woman, who officials said, was much smaller than 200-pound Belle Gunness. They had been murdered and their bodies stacked in the basement before the house caught fire.

After digging up the farmyard, eleven dismembered bodies were found, including Belle's adopted daughter who had vanished two years earlier. In the end, investigators ruled that Belle Gunness had died in the fire, however, many local residents suspected that she had engineered her own disappearance.

South Bend Tribune 11/19/1989

QUESTIONS

150. Which famous schnozzolla surprised the policemen at South Bend's Fraternal Order of Police picnic in 1959?

151. When did Notre Dame make its first appearance in the NCAA basketball tournament?

152. In 1923 the Bendix Corporation began manufacturing brakes after buying the American patent rights to a French 4-wheel braking system. What was the reason behind Vincent Bendix's interest in brakes?

153. What happened at Mishawaka's first Fourth of July celebration in the 1830's?

Courtesy of the South Bend Tribune
Jimmy Durante at the FOP Picnic

ANSWERS

150. After an appearance before 1,200 dealers at the Mobile Home Show, Jimmy Durante made an unscheduled stop at the FOP picnic. The outing was in full swing at the pistol range when the "schnozz" arrived at 10:45 p.m. The policemen quickly gathered around the piano to see the famous Durante and to hear him croak "Won't You Come Home Bill Bailey?"

South Bend Tribune 8/27/1959

151. Notre Dame first made it to the NCAA's in 1953. That year, their leading scorer was Dick Rosenthal, Notre Dame's Athletic Director from 1987 to 1995.

Notre Dame Program 10/6/1990

152. Vincent Bendix's father died in 1922 after being hit by a car with faulty brakes. Bendix vowed to devise a better braking system. He spent a year and $350,000 improving that French braking system before he introduced Bendix brakes in 1923.

St. Joseph Valley Record, Northern Indiana Historical Society, Fall 1990

153. The townsfolk expected to celebrate the Fourth of July with the help of a cannon that they had ordered from Detroit. It was shipped via the Great Lakes and then up the St. Joseph River to Mishawaka. It arrived three days late. Undaunted by the delay, the townspeople finally gathered with great anticipation to celebrate their first Independence Day. Unfortunately, when they lit the cannon, it exploded, showering smoke and shrapnel over the crowd. Three bystanders were injured.

Bridges, Janice, Indiana's Princess City, 1976.

QUESTIONS

154. After important games, MVP accolades are often given to those athletes who have contributed the most to their team's success. Who was named the Most Valuable Player after a Notre Dame basketball game against San Francisco in 1977?

155. More Presidents have come from the State of Virginia than any other; however, that's not the case with Vice Presidents. Indiana ranks number one in sending Vice Presidents to Washington. How many Vice Presidents of the United States have come from Indiana?

156. Why is Kosciusko County called the "Duck Capital" of the United States?

ANSWERS

154. NBC Sports named the Notre Dame student body as its Most Valuable Player after Notre Dame upset top-ranked and previously unbeaten San Francisco in a basketball game played at home in the Joyce ACC. With the encouragement and enthusiasm of its student body, Notre Dame had won over 80% of its home basketball games.

Notre Dame Basketball Guide 1992

155. Five Vice-Presidents have come from the State of Indiana. Schuyler Colfax, a South Bend resident, was elected Vice President during Ulysses S. Grant's first term (1868-1872) after serving in the U.S. Senate.

During Grover Cleveland's administration (1884-1888), Thomas A. Hendricks was the Vice President but died during his first year in office. He had served as the Governor of Indiana and had been elected to the U.S. House of Representatives and the U.S. Senate.

Charles Warren Fairbanks served with Teddy Roosevelt from 1905 to 1909. He ran again for Vice President in 1916 with Charles E. Hughes but was defeated.

President Woodrow Wilson served two terms with Thomas R. Marshall after being elected in 1912 and 1916. Marshall was the first to have actually been born in Indiana and was a past governor of the state.

J. Danforth Quayle was elected with George Bush in 1988 and served four years but the ticket was defeated in 1992. He had served in the U.S. House of Representatives.

South Bend Tribune 10/13/1992; Encyclopedia Americana

156. One company near Warsaw, Maple Leaf Duck Farm, produces about thirteen million ducks each year, which is 65 percent of the U. S. market. It also exports nearly 2 million ducks annually. As a by-product, the company generates about 2.5 million pounds of down and feathers that end up being used in pillows, comforters and beds. The ducks eat 3 million bushels of corn and and 21,000 tons of soybean meal each year.

Michiana Business, May 1992;
Corporate Communications, Maple Leaf Farms, Inc., July 1998

QUESTIONS

157. When was Mishawaka's first church founded?

158. Four out of Notre Dame's top fifteen all-time high scorers in men's basketball played in the same season. Who are they and what year did they play together?

159. How did the Ball-Band Company, now known as Uniroyal, get its name?

160. There is a "Bridge to Understanding" in our area which has a special meaning to many area residents. What does it mean?

Courtesy of Arthur D. Woodall, photographer, and
Mayor Robert C. Beutter, City of Mishawaka

Shiojiri Garden

ANSWERS

157. On July 24, 1834 the "First Presbyterian Trinitarian Society of the Village of St. Joseph Iron Works" was organized.

Northern Indiana Historical Society Calendar, 7/1992

158. Austin Carr, number one on the top-ten list, Bob Arnzen, seventh, Bob Whitmore, eighth, and Collis Jones, fourteenth, all played basketball for Notre Dame during the 1968-69 season. Their record that year was 20-7.

Notre Dame Sports Information 5/1999

159. Martin Beiger and his father owned Mishawaka Woolen Manufacturing Company which produced flannel and yarns. In 1887, he and Adolphus Eberhart developed an all-knit wool boot which proved to be an outstanding success. The boot had a black band around the top with a red ball on it. The names "Red Ball" and "Ball-Band" became registered trademarks of the company.

Bridges, Janice, Indiana Princess City, 1976.

160. The "Bridge to Understanding" is an actual bridge built in Merrifield Park in 1987 to commemorate the "Sister City" relationship between Mishawaka and Shiojiri, Japan. A 1.3 acre garden, designed by the Japanese landscape architect at Walt Disney World's Epcot Center, includes four small bridges, a dry garden representing the ocean and a teahouse pavilion.

Shiojiri Niwa brochures

QUESTIONS

161. Don't you wish we had mail service on Sundays, especially when waiting for something important to arrive? South Bend used to have Sunday mail deliveries. When were they discontinued?

162. Television is a relatively modern mode of communication. When and where was the first live UHF telecast made?

Courtesy of 22WSBT

An early telecast from WSBT

ANSWERS

161. Sunday mail service was discontinued on April 1, 1911.

Northern Indiana Historical Society Calendar 4/1992

162. On December 21, 1952, WSBT was the first UHF station in the world to have a live studio telecast. WSBT went on the air at 11:50 PM and just 55 minutes later showed ten minutes of news anchored by Justin Meacham and five minutes of weather with Bruce Saunders. Gilbert's Men's Outfitters presented UHF's first on-air commercial.

WSBT rushed to be the first station to telecast from their own studio just beating the station from Atlantic City, NJ. For the first month, regular programming was a test pattern except from 7:00 to 9:00 PM weekdays and 3:00 to 6:00 PM on Sundays. Network television didn't arrive in St. Joseph County until January 16, 1953 with the Dennis Day Show.

Less than one year later, on January 1, 1954, WSBT became the first station in Indiana to transmit in color with the Tournament of Roses Parade. Area residents got to see the show on a color monitor in WSBT's studio.

South Bend Tribune 10/26/1993

QUESTIONS

163. On January 27, 1932, Howard Woolverton, Secretary-Treasurer of Malleable Steel Range Mfg. Co., was kidnapped by a band of criminals. Woolverton and his wife had attended a show at the Granada Theater and then drove to George M. Studebaker's residence on Esther Street. About 11:00 PM, as they were returning to their home at 1246 East Jefferson Blvd., their car was forced to the curb and a gun-toting man jumped in announcing, "This is a stick-up."

He forced Woolverton to drive down Lincolnway West to a secluded spot five miles west of the city where Woolverton was forcibly removed from his car. Mrs. Woolverton was handed a ransom note and ordered to drive home slowly and to not read the note until she got there. At the intersection of Main and LaSalle, she stalled her car and seeing a policeman frantically reported the kidnapping. The ransom note said:

> "Do not notify police. You husband has been kidnaped (sic) for ransom. We want $50,000. Failure to comply with command means you will never see him again.
> "Now here is what to do. Wrap the money - good - in heavy paper. Get in the four-passenger Packard with the trunk on it that stays at the plant. Indiana license No. 20.
> "Go to Chicago Heights at eight P.M. Wednesday night. Start out on Highway No. 1. Do not drive over 25 miles an hour.
> "When you see a car behind you flash the lights ten times, drop the package on the pavement. If you do not get the signal by the time you get to Danville, turn around and come back the same way, not over 25 miles an hour. "This is your final instructions - no others. Do this, (or) you and some of the family will get hurt - BAD."

Twenty-four hours later, Woolverton returned home, haggard but unhurt. He refused to speak with reporters and it was speculated that a ransom had been paid, although the actual amount was never divulged. Who was the mastermind behind this kidnapping?

ANSWERS

163. In the January 1937 issue of American magazine, J. Edgar Hoover describes the Woolverton case as the first kidnapping ever attempted by "Machine Gun" Kelly (George Barnes) and his attractive wife and confederate, Kathryn Kelly. After finding out Woolverton did not have access to $50,000, the kidnappers released him but made him promise that he would pay them later. According to Mr. Hoover's version of the case, no money ever changed hands.

The pair later kidnapped an Oklahoma oil magnate who was held successfully for a $200,000 ransom. They were tracked down and captured by the FBI and both served life sentences in federal penitentiaries.

South Bend Tribune 1/27-29/1932, 3/2/1932, 1/16/1937

QUESTIONS

164. Who broke the 48-year old career yardage record held by George Gipp?

165. Seatbelts are known to save lives. In what year did all new Studebaker cars have factory installed seatbelts?

166. How many rows were there in Notre Dame's original Stadium?

167. Harry Albershart, alias "Red Ryder", was a famous Hollywood movie actor. He was born in Mishawaka, graduated from Mishawaka High School and attended the University of Notre Dame where he won varsity letters in football, basketball, and baseball. He appeared in Shirley Temple's "Stowaway" in 1936 and in "Charlie Chan at the Olympics" in 1937. In 1938 he got a part in his first Western and went on to star in approximately 60 more movies. He is even more famous to today's audiences for a part he played on television. Who did he portray on TV?

168. All football fans know that the offensive line is made up of very large athletes, often weighing 300 pounds each. They need to be that big in order to protect the quarterback from the also very big defensive line. What was the average weight of the "Seven Mules", Notre Dame's offensive line in 1924?

Courtesy <u>The Great Cowboy Stars of Movies & Television</u>

Allen "Rocky" Lane

ANSWERS

164. Gipp's long-standing record was beaten by Terry Hanratty, who passed for three touchdowns, ran for 55 yards, and was credited with 267 total offensive yards during the 1968 game against Illinois. Hanratty had played in 24 games to date and accumulated a total of 4,180 yards. From 1917 to 1920, Gipp played in 27 games and accumulated 4,110 yards in running and passing.

Notre Dame beat Illinois 58-8, after scoring eight touchdowns. They also broke a 36-year-old single game offensive yardage record by amassing a total of 673 yards. The old record was 664 yards, set in 1932 against the Haskell Indians.

South Bend Tribune 10/20/1968

165. Studebaker Corporation led the U.S. automobile industry by ordering seatbelts to be installed in all new cars in 1963.

South Bend Tribune 10/26/1993

166. There were 60 rows in Notre Dame's original stadium. The expanded Notre Dame Stadium, dedicated in 1997, has 80 rows with an official capacity of 80,012 fans.

1998 Notre Dame Football Media Guide

167. Baby Boomers would immediately recognize Harry Albershart's voice as that of "Mr. Ed", TV's talking horse. Under his stage name, Allan "Rocky" Lane, he spoke for "Mr. Ed" from 1961-66, after which he retired. He died in 1973.

South Bend Tribune 6/13/1993, The Great Cowboy Stars of Movies & Television

168. The "Seven Mules" average weight was 176 pounds, about the size of a kicker today.

Notre Dame Program 1992

QUESTIONS

169. Whose son was he? Bizarre cases of child snatching and murder seem to dominate the news today but in 1952, three families were claiming that an eight-year old Mishawaka boy was their son. Charley Joe Tipp, a third grade student at Ardmore School, was the center of this unusual tug-of-war. Do you know the story?

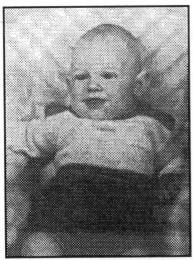
Baby Paul Jevahirian

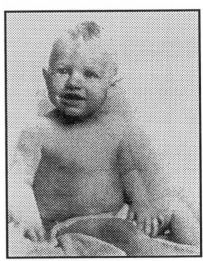
Baby Ronnie Thompson

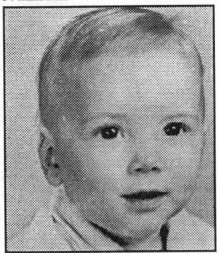
Baby Bobby Tipp

Photos courtesy of the South Bend Tribune

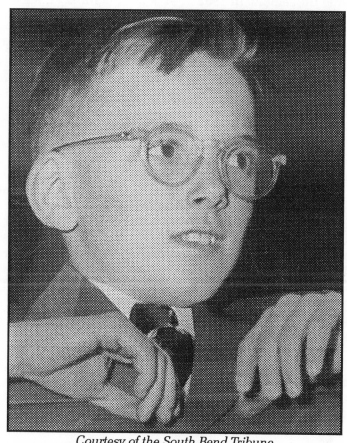

Courtesy of the South Bend Tribune

Nine-year-old Charley Joe Tipp

ANSWERS

169. On June 3, 1943, eleven-month old Paul Jevahirian was kidnapped from his home in Detroit, Michigan by a newly hired nursemaid. A little over a year later on October 7, 1944, twenty-month old Ronnie Eugene Thompson was kidnapped from his home in Dayton, Ohio, also by his newly hired nursemaid. In 1952 both of their families claimed that Charley Joe Tipp was their kidnapped son.

Charley Joe Tipp had been living in Florida with his mother and brother after his parents' divorce. Lois Tipp's erratic behavior had forced her husband to finally end the marriage and move back to Mishawaka where he was an X-ray technician at Bendix Aviation. On September 27, 1950 seven-year-old Bobby Tipp, Charley Joe's brother, was found murdered in his backyard. His mother, Lois Tipp, was accused of the murder but she was judged to be insane and committed to a mental hospital. Charley Joe's father, Robert Tipp, returned to Florida to regain custody of his son and bring him to Mishawaka to live.

Much to everyone's surprise, after a routine physical in the hospital, the doctors determined that Lois Tipp had never given birth to any children. So whose children were Bobby and Charley Joe?

Their father, Robert Tipp, said the boys were his. He was quoted as saying that Charley Joe "looks and acts like me and someone will have to prove that he's not my son". The authorities went searching for kidnap victims. They determined that Lois Tipp had probably kidnapped both the Jevahirian and Thompson babies. Each family then claimed that Charley Joe was their son. Even after exhuming Bobby Tipp's body, no positive identification could be made, but circumstantial evidence pointed to him as being the kidnapped Paul Jevahirian.

The Thompsons' filed a suit in March 1952 but the case was not decided until January 1953 after the assignment of a special judge and an eight-day trial. Dozens of pictures and hereditary links such as an unusual ear formation, blood type, a chin dimple and peculiar toes helped convince the judge that Charley Joe Tipp was really Ronnie Thompson. After the judge's decision, Charley Joe's "grandmother", who had cared for him while his "father" worked, released him to his birth mother causing tears to break out in the courtroom.

Charley Joe Tipp, by then nine and a fourth-grade student at Mary Phillips School, was moving to Dayton to live. With one decree, he acquired a new name, new parents, a new home, new school, new city and two new brothers. He was most excited about his new birthday because it meant that his gifts would arrive three months sooner. As he was leaving for Dayton, Ronnie/Charley Joe expressed a wish to return to Mishawaka to see his "Dad" and "grandparents", the only family he had ever known.

South Bend Tribune 3/5-7, 3/10-14, 6/1/1952; 1/7-9, 1/14-17/1953

QUESTIONS

170. Strike up the band! Notre Dame students and friends cheered loudly when the Notre Dame Victory March was played on December 4, 1928. Who was the leader of the band?

171. It's easy to guess that the largest town in St. Joseph County is South Bend. But, do you know the name of St. Joseph County's smallest incorporated town?

172. What is the longest winning streak in Notre Dame's football history?

173. Taverns have comforted travelers for many years. One, located in Southwestern Michigan, has been in continuous operation for over 160 years and is the oldest in the state. Do you know where it is located?

174. What amazing sight greeted travelers on the road from Elkhart to Culver in June 1993?

Courtesy of the South Bend Tribune

Two enormous statues being delivered to Culver

ANSWERS

170. Seventy-four-year-old John Philip Sousa led his band during two concerts at Notre Dame. They played Stars and Stripes Forever, the Notre Dame Victory March and other rousing numbers, including one accompanied by real fireworks. In between the concerts, Sousa presented a silver trophy to the Elkhart High School Band after they eliminated South Bend Central in the final round of a band contest.

South Bend Tribune 12/4/1928, 12/5/1928; South Bend News-Times 12/5/1928

171. Indian Village, on one square mile of land near Notre Dame, is the smallest incorporated town in St. Joseph County. It has all dead-end streets with about 60 homes, a population around 175, and no stores or traffic signals.

St. Joseph County at a Glance, 1993

172. The Irish, coached by Lou Holtz, had twenty-three consecutive wins in 1988 and 1989 including wins against nine of the top twenty teams. This broke the previous mark of twenty-one wins in a row set by Frank Leahy's teams between 1946 and 1948. With two ties included, Coach Leahy's 1946-1950 teams played 39 games in a row without a loss.

1998 Notre Dame Football Media Guide

173. In 1835, the Old Tavern Inn began as a stagecoach stop in Sumnerville and has been a restaurant or inn ever since. It's located 5 miles north of Niles off of M51 on Indian Lake Road.

South Bend Tribune 6/6/1993

174. Two enormous naked statues portraying ancient gladiators were trucked standing up on the back of a flat-bed truck. Although strategically covered with blankets, the light-green marble statues each weighing over 2,000 pounds stood seven-feet- tall. Shoe store magnate, Tom Spiece, bought the statues in Europe for delivery to his Lake Maxinkuckee home.

South Bend Tribune 6/17/1993

QUESTIONS

175. Almost everyone knows that the American buffalo nearly became extinct. In the late 1800's, they numbered between 20 and 40 million head, but mass slaughter by the white man over a period of a mere 20 years meant that by 1889 only 551 buffaloes were left alive. By the 1950's there were about 5,000 head, mostly in the western states. A local resident adopted 6 of these animals and brought them to this area in 1954. Who was he?

176. It must have been a shock to the train engineer when he looked through the dawn mists near Vandalia, Michigan and saw something heading right at him on February 28, 1893. He quickly reversed the engines, applied the air brakes and managed to pull to a stop. What was about to crash into the train?

177. Who wrote a column in the South Bend Tribune for nearly fifty years?

178. There were two small villages on opposing banks of the St. Joseph River when on February 17, 1838, the General Assembly combined them into one incorporated town called Mishawaka. What were the two original villages called?

179. The Notre Dame band is the oldest continuously existing college band in the nation. By 1887, when Notre Dame played football for the first time against Michigan, how old was the band?

ANSWERS

175. Homer Fitterling adopted the six buffaloes. For many years you could see them grazing along Indiana State Highway 2 west of South Bend.

South Bend Tribune 1/2/1955

176. A lone freight car loaded with barrels was hurtling down the track. It had been sitting on a sidetrack when the wind pushed it onto the main track. Because of ice on the tracks, it traveled right over the open switch picking up speed as it went. The single freight car crashed into the stopped train causing damage to the engine and scattering the barrels, but causing no injuries.

South Bend Tribune 2/28/1893

177. Etta Boswell Bowen wrote a society column called "In Colored Circles" which changed its name to "Neighborhood News" in the Sixties . When hired in 1919, she concentrated on the society news in the African-American community. At her retirement in she was honored by the Tribune for her long service.

South Bend Tribune 5/9/1993

178. The village on the south bank of the river was called St. Joseph Iron Works and was formed in 1833 right after the discovery of bog-iron deposits. Soon after, Indiana City was platted on the north side of the river.

South Bend Tribune 2/28/1993

179. The Notre Dame band was already celebrating its 41st birthday.

Notre Dame Program 10/12/1991

QUESTIONS

180. Twice a day, "Curly Top" would be there waving at the 20th Century Limited express trains as they traveled by her house in Elkhart. Every once in a while the cook would throw her a hollowed-out raw potato with a surprise inside. The potatoes contained autographed photographs, menus and notes from Hollywood stars like Spencer Tracy, Al Jolson, and Shirley Temple. Even former President Herbert Hoover wrote her a note.

"Curly Top" became famous. A book was written about her called *The Little Girl Who Waved* by Clara A. Ford; she went on a 3,000 mile autograph-signing trip on the 20th Century Limited in 1935; and she was named the honorary mayor of Detroit. Sadly, her mother died in 1938 and five months later her father abandoned her and her nine brothers and sisters. At the age of eleven, she was placed in an orphanage, first in Mishawaka and then in Fort Wayne. After she grew up, she became famous for something else. What was it?

181. Where was South Bend's first airport located?

182. Notre Dame football has generated a huge amount of fan interest. Notre Dame games are televised nationally each week; books are written about the teams and coaches; and the games and players are analyzed by newsmen, sportscasters and fans at length. Each winter there is a lot of speculation about which players will sign a national letter of intent to play for Notre Dame. The South Bend Tribune fielded so many calls about recruiting that they installed a hotline to answer the calls. How many calls were received by the recruiting hotline in January 1994?

Courtesy of Violet Schmidt Weitzman

"Curly Top" on the Twentieth Century Train

ANSWERS

180. "Curly Top", whose real name was Violet Schmidt Weitzman, became a pitcher for the Rockford Peaches and the Fort Wayne Daisies in the All-American Girls' Professional Baseball League. She was also an extra in the film "A League of Their Own".

South Bend Tribune 4/10/1939, 12/16/1940, 3/22/1946, 1/26/1992

181. The South Bend Municipal Airport was located six miles northeast of town at the corner of Brick and Fir Roads. John Kuespert, who was also assistant chief of police, was named the first airport manager and helped write the first ordinace regulating air travel. It was passed on April 22, 1929. The first airplane to land anywhere in South Bend was a Bleriot monoplane in 1911.

South Bend Tribune 1/20/1991

Courtesy of the Northern Indiana Historical Society

South Bend's first airport

182. In one month alone, 16,947 calls were made to the recruiting hotline.

South Bend Tribune 2/2/1994

Courtesy of Violet Schmidt Weitzman

Violet Schmidt fields the ball

QUESTIONS

183. In 1937 the Arrowbile arrived in South Bend for testing by the Studebaker Corporation. What was an Arrowbile?

From the collection of Studebaker National Museum, South Bend, Indiana

Arrowbile

184. During World War I local housewives were required to conserve food. On Mondays and Wednesdays they were expected to serve meals with no wheat in them, Tuesdays with no meat, and Saturdays with no pork. They were also asked to conserve fats and sugar. It was considered unpatriotic to break these rules because of the need to send more food to our soldiers in Europe. What unusual food did they use as a substitute for beef and pork?

185. Which Notre Dame basketball star became the first Irish player to average more than 20 points per game in a season?

Courtesy of the Studebaker National Museum

Alice Fay next to the Arrowbile

ANSWERS

183. The Arrowbile was the first combination airplane-automobile and was built by the Waterman Arrowplane Corporation from Santa Monica, California. It never went into actual production, however. Powered by a 6-cylinder Studebaker engine, it had a cruising speed of 105 MPH with a top speed of 120 MPH. Alice Fay, a movie actress, was photographed next to the Arrowbile.

Excerpted from Famous First Facts, © 1981 by The H.W. Wilson Company.

184. Whale meat became a substitute for beef and pork in many South Bend homes on meatless days. According to the Tribune, "whale meat when roasted can hardly be distinguished from the ordinary roast beef with the exception of a rather peculiar taste."

South Bend Tribune 2/7/1918

185. Dick Rosenthal, who later became Notre Dame's Athletic Director, averaged 20.2 points per game during the 1953-54 season.

Notre Dame Program 9/15/1990

QUESTIONS

186. In an 1893 edition of the Saturday Times, there is an advertisement titled "Manhood Restored". It said that this product was sold with a "written guarantee to cure all nervous diseases, such as weak memory, loss of brain power, headache, wakefulness, lost manhood, nightly emissions, quickness, evil dreams, lack of confidence, nervousness, lassitude, all drains and loss of power of the generative organs in either sex caused by overexertion, youthful errors or excessive use of tobacco, opium or stimulants which soon lead to infirmity, consumption and insanity". What was this product?

187. The Depression hit hard. Millions of people were out of work nationwide. There was no money to buy cars. Bad management decisions brought Studebaker Corporation to the brink of bankruptcy. A local company seeking payment of their $6,000 bill, sued the automaker. Who forced Studebaker into receivership?

188. Since 1935 the Heisman Trophy has been awarded each year to the most outstanding college football player in the country. How many Notre Dame football stars have won this trophy?

189. The first newspaper to be published in South Bend was The Northwestern Pioneer and St. Joseph Intelligencer. When did it publish its first issue?

ANSWERS

186. The advertisement was for a product called "Nerve Seeds" which could be obtained at two local establishments, Conley's Drug Store or Carey's Pharmacy, or shipped to the customer in a plain wrapper.

The Saturday Times 3/4/1893

187. The Edwards Iron Works of South Bend sued Studebaker on March 18, 1933. During the bankruptcy/receivership hearings, the judge appointed three members of the corporation as receivers: Paul Hoffman, Harold Vance, and Ashton Bean. Thanks to their help and that of the community, Studebaker was the only automaker in the United States to come back after being put into receivership during the depression.

On April 1, 1933, just two weeks after the judge's decision, there was a huge "Boost Studebaker" parade in South Bend. Local citizens were asked to be volunteer salesmen and the community's goal was to sell at least 100 Studebakers during the next thirty days. Even Notre Dame's president, Rev. John W. Cavanaugh, promised to sell one. Two weeks later he sold a new Rockne sedan to J. D. Oliver, son of James Oliver, founder of the Oliver Chilled Plow Works.

Assembly Line, Fall 1984

188. Seven Notre Dame football players have won the Heisman Trophy, more than at any other school. They are: Angelo Bertelli, Quarterback (1943); John Lujack, Quarterback (1947); Leon Hart, End (1949); John Lattner, Halfback (1953); Paul Hornung, Quarterback (1956); John Huarte, Quarterback (1964); and Tim Brown, Flanker (1987).

Notre Dame Football Program 9/9/1991

189. The first issue of the first newspaper in South Bend came off the press on November 16, 1831. The paper's name was later changed to St. Joseph Pioneer. It wasn't until 1865 that South Bend was incorporated into a town.

The Making of a Museum

QUESTIONS

190. In 1936 the silver jubilee of the South Bend Turnverein was held. Ten men had started this organization on June 13, 1861. In 1867 a drama group was formed with all plays being performed in German. Membership dues were twenty-five cents a month and physical exercises or "turning" was scheduled twice a week. What is this organization called today?

191. In 1935 the silver jubilee of this national event took place in South Bend. Exhibits were flown and trucked here from all over the United States. On the first day 125,000 spectators viewed a two-mile long parade led by the U.S. Army Second Infantry Band with 45 elaborate floats and 10 bands. The second day opened with a colorful bicycle parade of 100 children who then got to see the South Bend premiere of Jackie Cooper's new picture, "Dinky". Even with a downpour on the second day, over 10,000 persons visited the exposition. One of the exhibits was selected as "Miss South Bend". What was this big event?

192. This three-time world boxing champion retired in 1959 with a 55-0-1 record, winning mostly by knockouts. "What really worked for me was a double left hook followed by a right cross." Who was this professional boxer?

193. Two Notre Dame football players had unusual nicknames. One was called "Sleepy Jim" and the other the "Baby-Faced Assassin". Who were they?

Courtesy of the South Bend Turners

Founders of the South Bend Turnverein

ANSWERS

190. American Turners is the name of the organization that had it's 75th anniversary in 1936.

South Bend Turnverein

191. The twenty-fifth National Exhibition of Gladiolus sponsored by the American Gladiolus Society was held in South Bend in 1935.

South Bend Tribune 8/8, 8/18/1935; South Bend News Times 8/11, 8/17/1935

192. Phyllis Kugler retired after seven years of boxing, one as an amateur and six as a pro, at the age of 22 when her fiance made her choose between marrying him or continuing her boxing career. When she was 16, she began boxing under the name Phil Kugler for promoter, Johnny Nate, and participated in the "Friday Night Fights" until they got closed down because she was a woman. As a pro she held the titles for Bantam-weight, Featherweight and English champion. Her mother was unhappy with her choice of careers especially after Phil's nose was smashed flat in a title fight in Texas. While earning her world women's titles at three different weights, she got to travel across the country and appeared on television shows like "I've Got a Secret", "What's My Line", and "The Steve Allen Show". Now known as Phyllis McCormick and the owner of the Boutique Exchange, she has five children, nine grandchildren, and three great-granchildren.

South Bend Tribune 1/29/1994, interview with Phyllis McCormick

193. Jim Crowley, a member of the famous "Four Horsemen", was called "Sleepy Jim" and John Lautar, captain and All-American guard on the 1936 team, was the "Baby-Faced Assassin".

Notre Dame Program 10/26/1991

Courtesy of Phyllis Kugler McCormick

Phyllis Kugler

QUESTIONS

194. Without any warning, on February 7, 1943, these were banned. For one day no store in the country could sell them. What was banned and why?

195. When was northern Indiana's worst blizzard?

196. Six years after the arsenic was stored in the Courthouse attic, a young man found it and thinking it was chalk, shared it with his buddies. One of the youngsters took a large chunk home where two little girls ate it, becoming very ill. Quick medical attention saved their lives. What was the arsenic doing in the Courthouse attic?

197. In the springtime in the early 1850's, the Notre Dame band began serenading the students. What caused the concert to come to an abrupt end?

ANSWERS

194. During World War II, the government suddenly announced that shoes were going to be rationed and ordered that for one day, no shoes could be sold at all. Customers rushed to local stores but were told to come back the next day with stamp No. 17 from their sugar-coffee ration book.

Each resident would only be allowed to buy three pairs of shoes a year. House slippers, rubber boots and infants' soft-soled shoes were exempted from the rationing program but other "less essential" shoes, like women's evening shoes or men's patent leather shoes, were totally prohibited from being manufactured. Shoe rationing became neccessary because leather had to be shipped from overseas through submarine-infested waters. Much of the domestic leather was being used by the armed forces.

South Bend Tribune 2/8-9/1943

195. From January 25-27, 1978, forty inches of snow fell in the Michiana area. Winds gusting up to 55 miles per hour created ten to twenty foot drifts, closing roads and stranding thousands of travelers. The wind chill was recorded at almost 50 degrees below zero and visibility was reduced to zero.

South Bend Tribune 1/27-31/1978

196. In 1837, a Centre township farmer had been discovered with dies, base metal, arsenic, and a press for making counterfeit dollars. He was promised immunity for his testimony against four other men who were then put in jail to await trial. They eventually escaped and only one was recaptured. At the conclusion of South Bend's first counterfeiting case, some of the arsenic was sold to a local druggist and the rest, three pounds, was stored in the Courthouse attic.

South Bend Tribune 1/15/1989

197. The Notre Dame band began their musical serenade from rafts floating in the middle of St. Mary's Lake. The weather was good but the rafts took on water and began to sink. Band members were forced to abandon ship and swim to shore.

Notre Dame Program 10/12/1991

QUESTIONS

198. Have you seen the movie, "Hoosiers"? Based on a true story, it depicts a small town school winning the Indiana state basketball championship against much bigger schools. What area team accomplished a similar kind of victory?

199. Where was the first circuit court session held in St. Joseph County?

200. A British captain heard it being played in a Polish concentration camp during World War II. During the Vietnam War, American POWs were heard humming or whistling it. What was this catchy tune?

ANSWERS

198. The 1982 the Plymouth High School basketball team won Indiana's state championship by beating Gary Roosevelt in double overtime, 75-74. Although seven points behind in the fourth quarter, the team rallied and tied it up with Scott Skiles' basket at the buzzer. Skiles scored 39 points and currently plays for the Orlando Magic in the NBA.

On its way to the title, Plymouth also had a come-from-behind win against Elkhart Memorial, an overtime victory against Marion, and a big win against the Indianapolis Cathedral team led by 6'10" Notre Dame recruit Ken Barlow. During the regular season Plymouth lost only to LaSalle and then turned around to beat them decisively in the semi-state. Over 400 high schools, large and small, competed for the state title but this small town small-sized team brought home Marshall County's first state championship.

South Bend Tribune 3/21-28/1982

199. On October 29, 1832 the very first circuit court session was held in the barroom of Lily's Tavern on the west side of Michigan Street at Jefferson Boulevard.

Northern Indiana Historical Society Calendar 1993

200. The Notre Dame Victory March was first played in 1908 in Holyoke, Massachusets and it soon became known all over the country. Therefore, it shouldn't surprise you to learn that there were reports of the Notre Dame Victory March being heard in the Hanoi Hilton and other Vietnamese prison camps in place of forbidden national anthems. As one ex-POW said, "It was the only song that everyone knew."

Notre Dame Program 10/13/1991

About the Author

Andy Jones was born in Georgetown, British Guiana (now known as Guyana) and emigrated to the United States in 1952. She was raised in Connecticut where she became a naturalized citizen.

She has lived in South Bend, Indiana since 1974 and became very involved in the community and in her three children's activities. She also enjoys traveling, family reunions, and puttering in her perennial garden.

Author's Note

A portion of the proceeds from this book will be given to charitable organizations which may include, but not necessarily be limited to: Hospice, Junior Irish soccer fields, and Bosom Buddies, a breast cancer support group.

REFERENCES

Anderson & Cooley, South Bend and the Men Who Have Made It. South Bend: The Tribune Printing Co., 1901.

Ault, Phillip H. South Bend Remembers, A Newspaper History of Old South Bend. Decatur, Illinois: Spectator Books, 1977.

Ayres, William D., Ed. *"South Bend's Fugitive Slave Case, The Issue Was Freedom"*. South Bend: Michiana Magazine. South Bend Tribune, March 30, 1969.

Bleier, Rocky with Terry O'Neil. Fighting Back. New York: Stein and Day, 1980.

Blue and Gold Illustrated. Fan Action, Inc., Mishawaka, Indiana. references as noted in text.

Bridges, Janice. Indiana's Princess City, The History of Mishawaka 1832-1932. Mishawaka: The Heritage Press, 1976.

"Boost Studebaker Parade Shows Support in Dark Depression Days." Assembly Line. South Bend: Discovery Hall Museum, Fall 1984.

Brown, Edyth J. Story of South Bend. South Bend: South Bend Vocational School Press, 1920.

Bucher, Cecelia Bain. The Pokagons. Indianapolis: Indiana Historical Society Publications, Vol. 10 No. 5, 1933.

Chapman, Chas. C. History of St. Joseph County Indiana. Chicago: Chas. C. Chapman & Co., 1880.

Chicago Magazine. Primedia Intertec Publishing Corporation. Chicago, Illinois. references as noted in text.

Chicago Tribune. Chicago, Illinois. references as noted in text.

Detzler, Jack J. The Emergence of a City, South Bend 1920-1930. South Bend: Northern Indiana Historical Society, 1985.

Dooley, Agnes W. Promises to Keep. New York: Farrar, Straus and Cudahay, 1962.

Elbel, Mrs. Frederick. The Making of a Museum. South Bend: Northern Indiana Historical Society, 1965.

Encyclopedia Americana. Grolier Incorporated. Danbury Connecticut. references as noted in text.

Grant, Ulysses S. Memoirs and Selected Letters. Ed. Mary Drake McFeely and William S. McFeely. New York: Literary Classics of the United States, 1990.

Hall, Leda McIntyre, Ed. St. Joseph County at a Glance. South Bend: Institute for Applied Community Research Indiana University South Bend, 1993.

Historic Background of South Bend and St. Joseph County in Northern Indiana. South Bend: Daughters of the American Revolution, 1927.

Howard, Timothy Edward. History of St. Joseph County. Chicago and New York: Lewis Publishing Company, 1907.

Kane, Joseph Nathan. Famous First Facts. New York: H. W. Wilson Company, 1981.

Karst, Frederick A. *"A Rural Black Settlement in St. Joseph County, Indiana Before 1900"*. Indiana Magazine of History.

Merrill, Martha. *"St. Joseph County's Black Pioneers: A Survey."* South Bend: Old Courthouse News, Northern Indiana Historical Society, Fall 1969.

Michiana Business. Bureau of Business and Economic Research, Indian University at South Bend, South Bend, Indiana. references as noted in text.

Northern Indiana Historical Society Calendar: Dates in History. South Bend, Indiana. references as noted in text.

Notre Dame Football and Basketball Programs. University of Notre Dame. Notre Dame, Indiana. references as noted in text.

Notre Dame Football Guide. University of Notre Dame. Notre Dame, Indiana. 1984,1998. references as noted in text.

Playbill: The National Theatre Magazine. Playbill Inc., New York, NY. references as noted in text.

St. Joseph Valley Record. Northern Indiana Historical Society. South Bend, Indiana. references as noted in text.

St. Joseph Valley Register. South Bend, Indiana. 1845-1884, references as noted in text.

Saturday Times, The. South Bend, Indiana. 1889-1893, references as noted in text.

Shiojiri Niwa brochures: Shiojiri Niwa, Shiojiri Garden and "*A Bridge to Understanding*" A History of the Sister City Relationship Between Shiojiri City, Nagano Perfecture, Japan and Mishawaka, Indiana, United States of America.

South Bend's Historic Districts, Historic Preservation Commission of South Bend & St. Joseph County. City of South Bend, Indiana. 1998.

South Bend News Times. South Bend, Indiana. 1913-1934. references as noted in text.

South Bend Times. South Bend, Indiana. 1882-1913. references as noted in text.

South Bend Tribune. South Bend, Indiana. 1872-present. references as noted in text.

Sport. Petersen Publishing Company, Los Angeles, California. August 1988.

Sports Illustrated. Time Publishing Ventures, Inc., New York, NY. Fall 1991, pages 83-85.

Wolfe, Rebecca. "*The Splash and Splendor of Vincent Bendix.*" St. Joseph Valley Record. Fall 1990, Vol 3 No 2. South Bend: Northern Indiana Historical Society.

WSBT's Weather Calendar. WSBT, South Bend, Indiana. references as noted in text.

Young, C. E., ed. South Bend World Famed. South Bend: Handelsman & Young, Northern Indiana Historical Society, 1922.

INDEX
Items are referenced by Question Number

The trivia included in this book was compiled from newspapers, books and other periodicals. I'm already working on Volume II.

Interesting facts and unique people abound in this area. If you know an interesting story about local industry, prominent celebrities, unusual weather, strange criminal activities or Notre Dame trivia, please send it to me at:

Andy Jones
c/o and books
702 S. Michigan
South Bend, IN 46601

Order Form

If you would like to order additional copies of this book at $12.95 each plus $3.00 for postage and handling, fill out this order form and mail to:

and books
702 South Michigan
South Bend, IN 46601

I would like to order _____ *copies of* **LEGENDS AND LOSERS**

Name: _____

Address: _____

City, State, Zip: _____

Phone: (___) _____

Enclosed is $_____ $12.95 each plus $3.00 for postage and handling for each book. (Indiana residents add 5% sales tax). Make checks payable to: and books.